D0912646

Glimpses of Baptist Heritage

Glimpses
of
Baptist
Heritage

Claude L. Howe, Jr.

BROADMAN PRESS
Nashville, Tennessee

The articles previously published are:

"William Newton Clarke: Systematic Theologian of Theological Liberalism," *Foundations,* 6:123-135, April 1963.

"The Significance of the Formation of the Triennial Convention," *Southwestern Journal of Theology,* 6:5-14, April 1964.

"Baptist History in the Making," *The Theological Educator,* 2:53-66, October 1971.

"British Evangelical Response to the American Revolution: The Baptists," *Fides et Historia,* 8:35-49, Fall 1976.

"Christian Ordinances in Baptist Churches," *The Theological Educator,* 8:58-65, Spring 1978.

"The Charismatic Movement in Southern Baptist Life," *Baptist History and Heritage,* 13:20-27, 65, July 1978.

"The Call, Placement, and Tenure of Ministers," *Baptist History and Heritage,* 15:3-13, January 1980.

4265-59
ISBN: 0-8054-6559-6

Dewey Decimal Classification: 286.09
Subject heading: BAPTISTS—HISTORY

Library of Congress Catalog Card Number: 80-68798
Printed in the United States of America

Affectionately dedicated to

JOYCE HOWE

my wife

Preface

History may be defined broadly as what has happened in the past involving human beings. Humans are not isolated entities, however, so the definition of history by Penrose St. Amant as "the interaction of persons and impersonal forces against the background of divine providence" is a proper one. History does involve nature, people, and God; but only people really have a history. Nature is below history, though a person might formulate the history of some part of nature. (In other words, an individual might write a history of the butterfly, but a butterfly will never write the history of a butterfly.) God is above history, not confined to the limits of time and space. People, creatures of nature and creations of God, have a history and are aware of the fact. Thus, with feet planted in the present and facing the future, people consciously and unconsciously steal glances over their shoulders toward the past, recalling where they have been, hoping for guidance for where they are going. A historical consciousness is inherent in humanity.

The Christian faith declares that people are also finite and sinful. A glance backward, consequently, sometimes grows out of a desire to stay there. Then history becomes enervating, turning the individual or institution, "like Lot's wife," into a pillar of salt, an inactive mass. The salt has then lost its savor and is worthy only to be trodden underfoot. Those who long constantly for "the good, old days" fall inevitably into this category.

Sometimes the glance backward reflects only what one had determined beforehand to see. This involves a manipulation of history for selfish purposes where one is trying to *use* history rather than *learn* from history. Openness and objectivity are essential insofar as they are possible, though these must not be identified with unconcern. The backward glance is always partial and sometimes hasty, so the historian consults with others concerning what they have seen and constantly reexamines his own conclusions.

The Christian historian views history from a limited perspective because he is humán. He sees in history unlimited possibilities because he is Christian. He recognizes the universe as the sphere of God's activity. God acted in history in a series of mighty events. Through the incarnation God entered history in Jesus Christ for our redemption. God guides history in a purposeful fashion and will culminate history in his own good time and way. Thus, as Daniel Day Williams wrote, "the way history is viewed and written is always important for Christian thought because the Christian faith concerns the meaning of history." The study of history has always been serious business for the informed believer.

The series of essays brought together in this volume represent study of Baptist history from various perspectives for over two decades. Most of the essays have been published previously but where needed have been revised and updated. They do not represent an attempt to provide a chronological, fully formulated history of Baptists in America. In totality, however, they provide glimpses into most major developments in Baptist heritage and relate this heritage to contemporary concerns, particularly among Southern Baptists.

Special acknowledgment is made to editors of the following journals for permission to include essays published previously by them: *Baptist History and Heritage, Fides et Historia, Foundations, Southwestern Journal of Theology,* and *The Theological Educator.* Linda Kelm assisted immeasurably in typing the manuscript. A special note of thanks is given to my wife Joyce.

Contents

Introduction

The Protestant Reformation in England provided the context from which Baptist churches emerged early in the seventeenth century. A Reformation that began during the second quarter of the sixteenth century paralleled a similar movement on the European continent and found institutional expression as the Church of England. The church required uniformity in form, doctrine, and practice, visibly evident in episcopal church government, the Thirty-Nine Articles, and the Book of Common Prayer.

A Puritan element within the church expressed dissatisfaction with these developments, desiring further reform, especially in the "Romish" prayer book. They sought to purify the church through ecclesiastical and legislative processes, attacking abuses and advocating changes. When these efforts met with little success, a few Separatist churches appeared, justifying their separation from the "false" Church of England on grounds similar to those proposed by Anglicans in separating from Rome. Robert Browne formed such a church at Norwich about 1581 on the basis of a covenant. This was "reformation without tarying for anie." His writings defended a gathered church and congregational polity.

Another group appeared in London under John Greenwood and Henry Barrow, who attacked the false worship, ministry, membership, and discipline of the Church of England. The Separatists were persecuted severely and the London leaders put to death. Many Separatists fled to Holland and some of these constituted the Ancient Church in Amsterdam, where Francis Johnson became the most prominent leader. The Amsterdam congregation served, for a time, as a model by which other congregations were formed; but dissent and fragmentation compromised Separatism as a viable option.

Discussions continued into the seventeenth century concerning what constituted true churches, how they should be formed, essentials and nonessentials, the role of government, and so forth. John Smyth became an active participant, inquiring, "Is not the visible Church of the New Testament with all the ordinances thereof, the chief and principal part of the Gospel?" Smyth, an Anglican clergyman, developed Puritan sympathies while a student at Cambridge University and by early 1607 united with a Separatist group at Gainsborough, becoming their leader. The group soon emigrated to Amsterdam, Holland, where Smyth persisted in his search for spiritual worship by a true church based on biblical principles. By 1609, Smyth rejected infant baptism and constituted a church on the basis of believer's baptism by baptizing himself and his followers. This action initiated a series of conferences with the Waterlanders, a moderate Anabaptist group, after which Smyth concluded that baptism should have been secured from them. Smyth and most of his followers then sought membership with the Waterlanders, which was finally accomplished in 1615 (three years after Smyth's death).

Thomas Helwys and a few others resisted this effort and continued the church on its original principles. Smyth and his supporters were dismissed. The Helwys group formulated a confession of faith in 1611 that may be regarded as the first Baptist confession. The confession rejected Calvinism by defending a general atonement and the possibility of falling from grace. Distinctive Anabaptist views concerning Christology, ministry, magistracy, and oaths were likewise denied. In early 1612, the Helwys group returned to England, settling at Spitalfield near London. There they formed the first Baptist church on English soil. *The Mistery of Iniquity,* published by Helwys in 1612, defended absolute religious freedom; but Helwys was soon imprisoned and died by 1616. The church survived, however, and within a decade others had been formed at Lincoln, Tiverton, Coventry, and Sarum.

The General Baptist witness, proclaimed by Smyth and perpetuated through Helwys, persisted through the 1630s and flourished in the two decades that followed. Churches associated in various regions and issued confessions of faith. A General Assembly began meeting in 1654, and representatives from churches throughout the nation formulated a doctrinal statement in 1660 that became the Standard Confession of General Baptists.

General Baptists survived renewed persecution following the Restoration in 1660 and rejoiced in the toleration granted by William and Mary in 1689. By this time, however, the influence of rationalism and Socinianism pervaded the religious atmosphere in England. Matthew Caffyn, a prominent General Baptist messenger, first defended a Hofmannite Christology that compromised the humanity of Christ and then a Socinian view that undercut his deity. The General Assembly split twice, appealing primarily to the Standard Confession and Six Principles of Hebrews 6:1-2, neither of which addressed the issues.

The Wesleyan Awakening revitalized religion in England from about 1738. Dan Taylor, a convert of the awakening, identified with General Baptists in 1763. Their archaic practices and deviant Christology soon repulsed Taylor, however, who in 1770 led in forming the New Connection of General Baptists composed of his and a few other evangelical churches. Older General Baptist churches which did not unite with the New Connection for the most part became Unitarian. The New Connection flourished under the leadership of Taylor, numbering about seventy churches before his death in 1816. This fellowship merged into the British Baptist Union in 1891.

Particular Baptist churches developed somewhat later in England than those of General Baptists. Henry Jacob, a Puritan clergyman, established a semi-separatist church at Southwark, London, in 1616, after consulting with some prominent Puritan leaders. The congregation functioned apart from the parish churches but did not forbid members to attend or receive the sacraments in these churches. John Lathrop became pastor in 1624, after Jacob departed for the New World, and served the church for a decade. Some members, who rejected baptism by the parish churches, withdrew in 1630, as did others in 1633. Some of the latter received "a further baptism." Lathrop departed for the New World in 1634, after his release from imprisonment. Three years later (1637), the church called Henry Jessey, another prominent Puritan clergyman.

In 1638, six persons withdrew from the Jacob-Lathrop-Jessey church because they rejected infant baptism and joined with John Spilsbury in a church based on believer's baptism. Thus, by this time, at least one church existed in London based on believer's baptism, congregational government, and Calvinistic theology. The mode of baptism had not become an issue and was probably by affusion. Soon, however, Richard Blunt suggested that baptism in the New Testament had been by immersion. Those who agreed knew of no group in England which immersed believers but had heard about the Collegiants in Holland who had recently introduced the practice. Blunt, who spoke Dutch, was sent to Holland where he observed the practice. Upon his return early in 1642, Blunt immersed a Mr. Blacklock; and being immersed himself, they baptized their followers in this manner. Sources are not clear as to whether Blunt was immersed in Holland or London.

By 1644, seven Particular Baptist churches existed in London. Representatives from these churches formulated the First London Confession, a Calvinistic statement that required believer's baptism by immersion. The next year Henry Jessey and most of his church accepted such a baptism at the hand of Hanserd Knollys, another recent convert to Baptist views. With strong, capable leadership, Particular Baptists flourished during the next two decades. They formed associations in Wales (1650) and Ireland (1653), as well as several in England (Abingdon, 1652; Western, 1653; Midlands, 1655). William Kiffin and London Baptists provided communication and supported cooperation within the entire fellowship.

Particular Baptists endured persecution from 1660 to 1689. John Bunyan was jailed for twelve years for preaching the gospel. Other Christians, including Congregationalists and Presbyterians, also suffered. In this community of suffering these groups stressed areas of agreement. Particular Baptists formulated the Second London Confession in 1677, based on the Westminster Confession of Faith. Slightly revised in 1689, that rather strong Calvinistic confession became the most prominent among Baptists for a century and a half.

Baptists suffered from cultural isolation and denominational uncertainty during the eighteenth century. Also, a hyper-Calvinism, promoted by John Gill and others, hampered an evangelistic witness. Gill, the first Baptist theologian and an accomplished Hebrew scholar, defended "no offers of grace." He refused to address the ungodly, who should not be encouraged to trust Christ. The Wesleyan Awakening moderated this emphasis, however, so that by the time of Gill's death some Baptist leaders were questioning his approach. Andrew Fuller, pastor at Kettering, published *The Gospel Worthy of All Acceptation* in 1785, defending an evangelical Calvinism. William Carey, at Leicester in 1792, published *An Inquiry,* defending the Great Commission as binding on all people and proposing the formation of a missionary society. As a result a small group (twelve ministers, one student, one layman) met after the Fall Association in 1792, at Kettering and formed the Particular Baptist Missionary Society which sent Carey and others to India and elsewhere in the years that followed.

The evangelical theology of Fuller and the missionary zeal of Carey infused new life into Particular Baptists during the nineteenth century. They created organizations, formed colleges, and addressed issues to such an extent that their influence far exceeded their numerical strength. The success of prominent pastors such as Charles Haddon Spurgeon at the Metropolitan Tabernacle in London and Alexander Maclaren in Manchester enhanced their image. An organization formed in 1813 developed into the British Baptist Union which provided a framework for the merger with General Baptists in 1891 and for a united Baptist witness in England and Ireland since that time.

Baptists in America date their beginnings from 1639 when Roger Williams accepted believer's baptism and then baptized about ten others, forming at Providence, Rhode Island, the first Baptist church in the New World. John Clarke, preacher and physician, formed a second church at Newport, Rhode Island, about 1644. Both these churches began as Particular or Calvinist bodies but divided in the 1650s when General or Six Principle groups withdrew to form distinct fellowships. Thus, the theological divisions existing in England persisted in New England. Likewise, Seventh Day Baptists from England emigrated to Newport, where in 1671 a church of this persuasion was formed.

A policy of religious uniformity accompanied by persecution of dissent also persisted in the New World, as nine of the thirteen colonies established state churches. Persecution was particularly severe in New England. Williams attacked the policy in *The Bloudy Tenent* (1644) and other writings, as did Clarke in *Ill Newes from New England* (1652).

After twelve years in England, Clarke succeeded in securing a charter for Rhode Island that established "a lively experiment" guaranteeing absolute religious freedom. In spite of difficulty, Baptist immigrants from the British Isles and converts in America succeeded in forming churches at Rehoboth (1663) and Boston (1665) in Massachusetts. By 1700, some ten Baptist churches existed in New England.

A policy of religious toleration in the Middle Colonies assisted Baptists in establishing a witness around Philadelphia in Pennsylvania and New Jersey. As early as 1684, Thomas Dungan, a native of Ireland, settled at Cold Spring, Pennsylvania, and formed a small church that survived for a time (until 1702). Elias Keach established a more permanent church at Pennepack (later Lower Dublin) in 1687-1688. The son of the prominent English pastor Benjamin Keach and "a very wild spark," Elias was baptized and ordained by Dungan after a brief imposture as a minister. He preached in the area for about three years, then in East Jersey, but returned to England in 1692. Other preachers, including Thomas Killingsworth from England and Thomas Griffiths from Wales, constituted churches also. In 1707, five of these churches formed the Philadelphia Baptist Association, the first and most influential association in America. By 1715, there were nine churches with a total membership of about 500. These churches accepted the 1689 English Baptist Confession which, with slight additions, was published by the association in 1742 as the Philadelphia Confession of Faith. The association eventually encompassed churches from New York to Virginia and became a model for establishing associations in other areas.

Only one Baptist church was planted in the South during the seventeenth century. William Screven of England arrived in the New World by 1668 and five years later purchased land in Kittery, Maine, which remained his home for over twenty years. He married into a prominent family and became an important figure in the community. In 1681 Screven was baptized in the Baptist church at Boston. The next year (1682) this church ordained him and assisted in constituting a church at Kittery.

Screven settled in South Carolina in 1696, becoming the first pastor of a Baptist congregation at Charleston. The church maintained contact with Particular Baptists in England and New England and numbered about ninety members in 1708. General Baptists formed the earliest church in Virginia under the leadership of Robert Norden (1714) and in North Carolina with Paul Palmer (1727); but inadequate leadership and Calvinizing activities sponsored by the Philadelphia Association weakened these churches. Virtually all of the General Baptist churches became Calvinistic or ceased to exist so that eventually a mild Calvinism prevailed in most Southern churches.

The First Great Awakening transformed Baptist life in America. The Presbyterian Gilbert Tennent, Congregationalist Jonathan Edwards, and Anglican George Whitefield spearheaded a resurgence of religion that spread throughout the colonies and influenced virtually every religious group. Prominent clergymen and pious laymen emphasized personal conversion, studied Scripture, prayed fervently, and itinerated freely. Congregationalists in New England fragmented in the aftermath of the Awakening, and numerous Strict or Separate congregations were formed by those favoring the revivalist approach. Resistance from churches of the Standing Order and discussions about religious freedom, a regenerate church, and believer's baptism by immersion resulted in many of these churches and members becoming Baptist, giving rise to the Separate Baptists.

The experience of Isaac Backus was typical as he was converted during the early Awakening, joined the Congregational church at Norwich, Connecticut, withdrew with others to form a Separate church, and in 1748 became pastor of a similar body in Middleborough, Massachusetts. In 1751, Backus rejected infant baptism and was immersed by a Baptist preacher but for five years allowed others to baptize infants in his church. Backus formed a Separate Baptist church at Middleborough in 1756, which he served for half a century while becoming the voice of Baptists in New England on behalf of religious freedom. The extensive historical endeavors of Backus likewise promoted the cause of freedom. Baptist churches in New England increased to 325 by 1790. By that time distinctions between Separates and Regulars had virtually disappeared.

Separate Baptists extended into the South also. Shubal Stearns and Daniel Marshall experienced conversion in New England and accepted Baptist views before settling with their families and friends at Sandy

Creek, North Carolina, in 1755. With the Sandy Creek church as a base, Separates spread through North and South Carolina, Virginia, and into Georgia. The Sandy Creek Association formed in 1758 encompassed all their churches until 1770, when the churches were distributed into three regional bodies. Frequent contact with Regular Baptists with whom they shared in the struggle for freedom encouraged efforts for unity so that a formal merger could be culminated in Virginia in 1787 and in other areas with less formal actions. The merger aided in confirming Baptists as evangelistic churchmen, with the Separates contributing a concern for evangelism, biblicism, and freedom and the Regulars providing a concern for organization, cooperation, and education.

Baptists expanded and matured in the new nation but faced unprecedented opportunities and challenges. Having developed a denominational consciousness and secured religious freedom, they addressed an unlimited frontier and world mission challenge. The formation of a national organization in 1814 evidenced the new sense of identity and commitment but as some forces encouraged unity, others nurtured division. Baptists remain the largest evangelical fellowship in the nation. The nature of problems faced by them shifted late in the nineteenth century, and the number multiplied in the twentieth. Once again Baptists struggle for a clear sense of identity and search for viable goals in an increasingly secular, pluralistic society. The chapters that follow provide glimpses into some of these developments and should be understood and interpreted within the broad, historical framework that has been sketched.

The first chapter focuses upon the life, work, and influence of the pioneer Baptist historian in America and provides reflections upon the historical discipline. The second notes the critical support provided by Baptists in England, at the time when the thirteen colonies were securing their freedom. The common heritage of all Baptist groups in America is stressed in the third chapter with a discussion of the significance of the first national organization. Chapter four documents that tendencies toward both separation and cooperation have always existed in Baptist life and traces some results of these tendencies for organizational life in America. The fifth chapter describes changes in the life of one Baptist influenced by the complex of forces at work in American religion during the late nineteenth and early twentieth centuries. Chapters six and seven provide insight into the Baptist views of ministry and the ordinances, and the eighth assesses the influence of the charismatic movement on Southern Baptists. The final chapter deals with critical issues in Southern Baptist life today, attempting to relate the Baptist heritage to contemporary problems.

1

Baptist History in the Making

Contemporary historians have devoted a great deal of attention to the theory and practice of their discipline. One influential report on the subject outlines some basic premises involved in all historical study. The first premise refers to the historian as "one of the guardians of the cultural heritage of mankind" and "an interpreter of the development of mankind."[1] Premise six states that "every written history, particularly that covering any considerable area of time and space, is a selection of facts made by some person or persons and is ordered or organized under the influence of some scheme of reference, interest, or emphasis-avowed or unavowed-in the thought of the author or authors."[2] These premises indicate the importance and the vulnerability of the historian.

The historian functions as a guardian of culture while participating actively in the culture. He interprets development while sharing in the developmental process. His selection and arrangement of materials reflect a commitment concerning what is meaningful in the past for the present or future. For these reasons, the report concludes that "written or spoken history is to be best understood not only by analysis of its structure and documentation, but also by a study of the possible attitudes arising from the life and circumstances of the author."[3]

Morgan Edwards contributed more toward collecting and preserving Baptist historical materials in Colonial America than any other individual. Directly and indirectly his influence encouraged historical endeavors that continued throughout much of the nineteenth century. Contemporary historians acknowledge their dependence upon his assertions about Colonial Baptists at many points. The entire denomination regards him as their first historian in America. "The historian who survives," observes Herbert Butterfield, "seems to be the one who in some way or other has managed to break through into the realm of enduring ideas or gives hints of a deeper tide in the affairs of men."[4] Without a doubt, Edwards survives in influence among Baptists today. The present study, therefore, will seek an understanding of his significance not only through an analysis of "structure and documentation" but also in terms of his "life and circumstances." Hopefully in the process some "enduring ideas" or "hints of a deeper tide" may break through.

Edwards's early life and circumstances conditioned the future historian remarkably for his career in America. Born May 9, 1722, in the Parish of Trevethin and County of Monmouth, Wales, he attended a village school at Trosnant, near the place of his birth. Reared in the Church of England, he became a Baptist in 1738, surrendering to the ministerial call shortly thereafter. Bernard Foskett, a prominent Baptist educator, directed his higher studies at Bristol Academy, after which Edwards accepted a small pastorate in Boston, England, where he lived for seven years. Nine years of service followed at Cork, Ireland, during which time he was ordained (June 1, 1757). Here the Baptist preacher married Mary Nun, by whom two children survived infancy. A brief pastorate at Rye, England, immediately preceded his coming to Philadelphia, where he served for about a decade before relinquishing pastoral duties.

A farewell sermon delivered before the congregation at Rye betrays mixed emotions about the decision to come to America. "The quitting my native country, friends, and relations (probably) for ever is grievous," he said, "and yet after a mature consideration; and consulting my honoured friends; and brethren in the ministry, it appears to me I ought to go."[5] Edwards's ministry had been a happy and successful one attended by large crowds, substantial offerings, additions to the church, and genuine spiritual growth. An appreciative congregation beseeched him to remain, even promising a liberal increase in salary. Impelled by a sense of duty, Edwards departed for the new land, but fond regard for his native country never diminished.

Edwards possessed a cosmopolitan outlook and scholarly abilities that distinguished him immediately from most American Baptist ministers. "He had attained a remarkable ease of behavior in company,"

William Rogers observed, "and was furnished with something pleasant or informing to say on all occasions."[6] A capable linguist, Edwards commented often that "Greek and Hebrew are the two eyes of a minister; and that translations are but commentaries, because they vary in sense as commentators do."[7] His reaction to certain pulpit discourses evoked an observation that "an American, with an English Grammar in his hand, a learned friend at his elbow, and close application for six months, might make himself master of his mother tongue."[8] After the College of Philadelphia awarded him a Master of Arts degree in 1762, Edwards conducted services regularly while wearing a master's gown.[9]

The Baptist community in America displayed few of the characteristics attributed to Edwards. A small constituency with little visible unity was scattered throughout the colonies. Three local associations and a Latin Grammar School constituted organized Baptist life beyond the local churches. Baptists distinguished themselves from one another with such designations as General and Particular, Regular and Separate, First-day and Seventh-day, British and German. Only in Rhode Island did they enjoy absolute religious freedom. Their ministers, for the most part, were untrained and unpaid. The First Great Awakening had infused new life into the fellowship, however, and the Revolutionary War soon provided greater freedom. For over three decades, therefore, Morgan Edwards reminded a denomination engaged primarily in building for the future that valuable insights could be gained from recalling the past.

The first American Baptist historian would have disagreed sharply with Hegel's remark that "we learn from history that man learns nothing from history."[10] Albert Outler more nearly expressed Edwards's sentiments in his presidential address before the American Society of Church History: "Our interest in plausible narratives of actual events stems from their power to help us identify ourselves with other men across the gaps of time and memory and to participate, in some measure, in their experience of the grandeur, the misery, and the radical ambiguity of life."[11]

Despite the contrasts noted previously, Edwards identified quickly with American Baptists after his arrival on May 23, 1761. From that time until his death, the Welsh preacher promoted unselfishly the Baptist interest, which was, in his judgment, "the interest of Christ above any in

Christendom."[12] Minutes of the Philadelphia Association for 1761 refer repeatedly to the new pastor, and they also record information furnished by him. Appointed to assist in maintaining the records, Edwards reflected his historical concern by inserting a statistical table which described the condition of the churches for the year. It included data "collected partly from their Letters to the Association, and partly from private information."[13] Five years later, with Edwards as "the moving cause," the association authorized the printing of its annual minutes.[14] A year before his death, the Baptist historian presented to the association bound copies of its minutes from the beginning until that time. Edwards played a major part, therefore, in preserving for Baptists the records of their first and most influential association in America.

The 1761 Philadelphia Association requested also that Edwards and Peter Vanhorn revive and maintain a correspondence with the Board of Particular Baptist Ministers in London. Previous correspondence had resulted in John Gill's recommending Edwards for the Philadelphia pastorate. "We greet you well: and, as a part of that community, in the British Dominions, (whereof you have in some sort the superintendence,) we offer you our acquaintance," began the letter, "and solicit a share of your public care and friendship."[15] Demonstrating that the last clause implied more than a sympathetic attitude, Edwards appealed for funds for Hopewell Academy and the associational library. At the first associational meeting which he attended, the Philadelphia pastor displayed concern for Baptist history and denominational fellowship, recognizing also the essential role which ministerial education played in these matters.

Edwards projected a major historical production entitled "Materials Toward a History of the American Baptists, in XII Volumes." Volume One, which dealt with Pennsylvania Baptists, appeared in print during 1770. Volume Two traced the history of New Jersey Baptists and was published in 1792. Two additional volumes, published posthumously, presented Baptist developments in Rhode Island (1867) and Delaware (1885). Additionally, Edwards's historical materials for Virginia, North Carolina, South Carolina, Georgia, and Maryland are available in manuscript form. These works represent years of painstaking research, miles of arduous travel, and thousands of personal interviews. Without them, the present knowledge of Colonial Baptist history would be sizably reduced.

"History originates in curiosity about the past," Sidney Mead observed recently, and such curiosity is "manifested in questions."[16] The questions change with changing times, for "people want to know how they 'got that way' in order to understand their present situation in such fashion as to suggest what they can and ought to do."[17] Thus Mead could state that "every written history is essentially an assertion in the form of a thesis that constitutes an answer to a question about the past. The totality of such assertions constitutes the body of historical knowledge."[18]

Vital questions that challenged Baptist leaders throughout Edwards's lifetime involved denominational unity. How had Baptist churches originated and developed apart from one another? What could be done to encourage cooperation among them? In the first volume of his history of American Baptists, Edwards indicated that his motives for collecting and publishing historical materials were related directly to these questions. "The motive to the first was, a desire to know the American Baptists; the motive to the other was, an equal desire to make them known one to another." Edwards designated his "grand motive," however, as a "solicitude to unite them together and to settle some useful means of intercourse and familiarity between their churches."[19] Baptists could overcome many of their differences, he believed, by becoming better acquainted personally and by studying their history. For this reason, Edwards never considered his historical endeavors as isolated activities. He saw them as genuine contributions toward accomplishing a central purpose, namely denominational unity in America.

The route chosen provided many difficulties, for Edwards faced a constituency which had to be convinced about the importance of history as well as unity. Rejoicing late in life because of some "spirit of history" and "other refinements" evident among Baptists, the historian recalled several early experiences. "What good will your history do?" inquired individuals from whom better was expected. "You take much pains to no purpose! You are numbering the people like David." "Such talk prognosticated no great attention to his book," Edwards remarked, "nevertheless he printed it; and lost about thirty pounds by the edition."[20]

The Revolutionary War complicated the situation further because many church records were destroyed, a volume prepared for the press burned with his house, a hundred copies of his first volume were confiscated, and his personal freedom was circumscribed. "But though he suffered such losses, and, for years, stood alone in the undertaking," commented Edwards about himself, "yet was he not discouraged; so convinced was he of the necessity of a history of the American Baptists."[21]

Edwards provided concrete suggestions in 1770 for implementing denominational unity among American Baptists. Basically, his scheme proposed that local Baptist churches unite into provincial associations which would then participate in a national fellowship centered around the Philadelphia Association. More specifically, however, the plan recommended five phases. First, the Philadelphia Association should be embodied by charter. Its membership should include one person from each provincial association. Second, a preacher should be appointed and supported to visit all the churches as an evangelist. Third, the nature of Baptist associations should be publicized since they differ from all similar assemblies. Fourth, Baptist churches from Nova Scotia to Georgia should become acquainted with one another. Edwards anticipated that his *Materials* could contribute in this area. Fifth, the union should be comprehensive enough to include all Baptist churches of reputable character even though they differed on unessential points of faith or order.[22] "Practising believer's baptism is our denominating article. If this be taken away we shall differ from the Independents in no point whatever," Edwards declared. "And the one thing which distinguishes us from every sect of Christians, and made, and keeps us a separate and distinct body of people," he continued, is "one would think, a sufficient ground of union among ourselves, excepting only where this 'truth is held in unrighteousness.' "[23] A national Baptist organization became a reality about two decades after Edwards's death, but the first serious proposals circulated in his history about fifty years earlier.

Because of his interest in ministerial education, Edwards likewise suggested in 1762 the establishment of the first Baptist college. Al-

though many Baptists discouraged such a project because of "an unhappy prejudice against learning,"[24] success attended the venture. Initially located at Warren, Rhode Island College was chartered in 1764 as a
nonsectarian institution. But Edwards reminded his readers that "the
baptists only, made a motion for it, the baptists only, gathered money to
endow it; the head of it and about two-thirds of the fellows and trustees
must ever be of that denomination."[25] A fellow of the college from its
founding, the Philadelphia pastor undergirded the school with financial
and moral support during its formative years. Obtaining a leave of
absence for two years from his church, Edwards solicited endowment
funds in Europe. Local pastors supplied the Philadelphia pulpit but were
paid out of his salary. Besides securing many books, including the thirteen hundred volume library of Dr. Richards, Edwards collected almost
nine hundred pounds sterling. His mission "succeeded pretty well," he
said, "considering how angry the mother country then was with the
colonies for opposing the stamp act."[26]

In an autobiographical sketch, Edwards indicated the prominent position that Rhode Island College occupied in his thinking. "He laboured
hard to settle a baptist college in Rhode Island government and to raise
money to endow it which he deems the greatest service he had done or
hopes to do for the honour of the baptist interest."[27] Edwards actively
solicited funds, collected books, enlisted students, and attended meetings until 1789. He relinquished his fellowship at that time because age
and distance rendered him incapable of attending the corporation meetings. With the possible exception of President Manning, no person sacri-
ficed more unselfishly than Morgan Edwards during the early years to
insure the success of the first Baptist college in America.

Edwards pursued his interests in Baptist history, denominational
unity, and ministerial education within a pastoral context until July 8,
1771. The Philadelphia pastorate prospered under his leadership for
several years, as the membership increased steadily, a new edifice was
constructed at a cost of 2200 pounds, and a harmonious fellowship
prevailed. But the cordial relationship apparently deteriorated during
the pastor's extended absence in England. Furthermore, on January 1,
1770, Edwards preached from the text "This year thou shalt [surely] die"
(Jer. 28:16). Convinced that the text applied to him, the pastor predicted

that his death would come within the year. Combined with his outspoken individualism, these factors provoked serious problems and his eventual resignation.

On the other hand, numerous incidents involving the congregation before and after Edwards's pastorate indicate internal dissension of long standing, thereby forbidding one to conclude that all the difficulties stemmed from the pastoral side.[28] Edwards continued preaching in Philadelphia until the church obtained another minister (William Rogers). Edwards purchased a plantation in Pencader, Delaware, and moved there in 1772 with his family. Several destitute churches benefited from his preaching before the Revolutionary War, but Edwards retained his church membership at Philadelphia and never accepted pastoral responsibilities again.

Difficulties that existed between Edwards and the Philadelphia church did not diminish his influence in the association. Most contemporary Baptist pastors agreed with Francis Pelot that charity from the church might have served as "a means of preserving the usefulness of a talented man,—a man who has scarce his fellow in a warm attachment to the Baptist interest."[29] Besides being elected in 1771 as associational clerk and messenger to the Warren Association, Edwards was selected as the first associational evangelist.

Although frequently represented as a missionary enterprise, this selection should be understood as a segment of the program described previously for promoting denominational unity. Rather than riding a circuit in destitute areas winning converts and establishing churches, Edwards visited existing Baptist churches and associations in the South for the purpose of strengthening a denominational consciousness. The Philadelphia body, which had exchanged messengers and correspondence with the Warren and Ketocton Associations for several years, anticipated a similar response from the Congaree, Kehukee, Sandy Creek, Rapid Anne, and Charleston Associations in 1773 as a direct result of Edwards's labors.[30] Since these associations encompassed Baptists with varied theological and ecclesiological outlooks, he must have emphasized a comprehensive basis of cooperation.

The Baptist historian also collected historical information by consulting records, interviewing individuals, and observing procedures and facilities. After Edwards visited Charleston, Oliver Hart referred to him as "a great, good man; firmly attached to the Baptist interest, to promote which he cheerfully encounters all difficulties."[31] Similar testimonies followed his visits elsewhere. The Philadelphia Association expressed appreciation for his success, but Edwards declined his reappointment for another year.

When the Revolutionary War approached, Edwards's influence among Baptists declined somewhat because of his outspoken Tory sentiments.

For any person to have been so marked out in those days was enough to bring on political opposition and destruction of property, all of which took place with respect to Mr. Edwards, though he never harboured the thought of doing the least injury to the United States by abetting the cause of our enemies.[32]

In accordance with legal requirements, Edwards desisted from preaching throughout the conflict. His presence at the Philadelphia Association is not recorded after 1775 until 1791. One son became a British Army Officer and the other served as an American sailor. His wife died, after which he married a Mrs. Singleton of Delaware, but Edwards survived her also. These factors do not justify his yielding to intoxicants, but they arouse sympathetic understanding for one previously acclaimed "a gentleman of most exemplary morals and piety."[33] At one time Edwards declared, "Surely if any creature of God were not good rum would be it."[34] Restored to good standing after being under church censure for four years, the Baptist historian maintained thereafter a high standard of Christian conduct. Before his death Edwards "occasionally read lectures in divinity" at various places but "could never be prevailed upon to resume the sacred character of a minister."[35]

For over three decades in changing roles and under varied conditions, the first American Baptist historian collected, structured, and corrected his historical *Materials*. Commenting on his methodology, Edwards stated that "materials toward a history cannot be too particular: the Baptist interest in America is too young to admit a historical narrative which shall be entertaining; it would be like the history of a child."[36] Instead of producing interpretive narratives, the pioneer historian strove for particularity, envisioning that later historians would utilize his documents in constructing narrative accounts of Baptist developments. Uniformly, Edwards listed the churches of a province individually, located them specifically, and identified their branches. He designated also the distance and direction from Philadelphia and provided detailed information about the physical property. Then followed a description of the manner of origin, faith and order, remarkable events, past pastors, and present status of each church.

The method chosen probably accounts in large part for Edwards's high esteem among Baptist historians and his relative obscurity elsewhere. "This method gained my approbation at first," he wrote in 1790, "and after more than twenty years attention it retains the preference it gained."[37] But Edwards recognized that his methodology could not guarantee perfect results. "No person (except he should try the experiment) can imagine the difficulty, if not impossibility of correctness and accuracy in such an undertaking as I and others have been engaged in," he said. "Truth is the daughter of time. By it have mistakes in all histories been corrected."[38]

Distinguished as a capable historian, Edwards should be remembered also as a promoter of historical research and writing. At his suggestion, Isaac Backus began his extensive research in this field.[39] After the former gathered materials among Eastern churches as far as New Hampshire, "such of them as he had put in any order he sent to Mr. Backus."[40] Pursuing the theme of religious freedom, Backus became the "standard author in Baptist history" until David Benedict published his works.[41]

Edwards rode three thousand miles collecting materials about the Southern churches with the intention of publishing them. But when John Leland anticipated writing a history in this area and requested access to his materials "those papers were sent to him with great good will."[42] Leland published the *Virginia Chronicle,* which Robert Semple used in formulating his classic study in 1810 of Virginia Baptists.

In a postscript to his second volume, Edwards exhibited his abiding interest in Baptist history. "The history of them in Delaware state is obtained already; and will be sent to the press as soon as a sufficient number of subscribers offer," he said. "The author cannot expect to see it printed, because of an *asthma* and *atrophy,* which hurry him out of the world." The historian noted, however, that he would "leave the manu-script in such hands as will do justice to it and the public: the price will be about a quarter of a dollar."[43]

His real interest centered at another point. "It is presumed that Dr. Jones, of Pennepek, will soon make a tour through New York, to gather materials towards a history of the Baptists in that state; and perhaps thro' Maryland and Pennsylvania. If not, some other public spirited per-son will do it, as a taste for history and other refinements hath arisen to some height, even among the American Baptists."[44] Succeeding gen-erations have acknowledged gratefully that Morgan Edwards played a strategic role in bringing these changes about.

Besides his historical productions, the Welsh preacher published sev-eral other volumes. Intended as a church discipline, "The Customs of Primitive Churches" gained little acceptance among his contemporaries. Nor did his treatises on the millennium, public worship, and last-novel-ties exert much influence. Upon his departure from England (1761), at the ordination of Samuel Jones (1763), and on New Year's day, 1770, Edwards preached sermons that also appeared in print. Partially be-cause of the prediction concerning his death, the last one passed through four editions.

All of these works reveal that Edwards's interests were practical and exegetical rather than theological. Firmly committed to the authority of Scripture, which should be interpreted "in a literal sense, except when that leads to contradiction or absurdity,"[45] he emphasized the priest-hood of all believers. By conviction a Calvinist, he "seldom meddled with the five polemical points; but when he did, he always avoided abu-sive language."[46] His theological cosmopolitanism created problems occasionally, however, for charges of Arminianism and Universalism were leveled at him. On the latter point, William Rogers remarked that though Edwards was not a Universalist, "he professed a great regard for many who were, and he would sometimes take their part against violent opposers, in order to inculcate moderation."[47] But moderation was not the order of the day, hence the Welsh preacher often suffered abuse because of personal association with those of divergent theological views.

Edwards was present at the Philadelphia Association in 1794 for the last time. He faced the experience of death which he had anticipated for twenty-five years on January 28, 1795, at Pencader, Delaware. By prior request, William Rogers preached Edwards's funeral sermon based upon the text, "By honour and dishonour, by evil report and good report: as deceivers, and yet true" (2 Cor. 6:8). Aware of some dishonor, evil reports, and charges of deception, posterity has chosen nevertheless to remember Morgan Edwards primarily as a man of honor, good report, and truth.

The historical discipline has changed repeatedly since Morgan Edwards structured the first Baptist history. Several scholars during the past decade described "shifting trends"[48] and "changing perspectives"[49] which dominated the interpretation of American religious history at various times. "I have been surprised again and again to find how the past keeps changing even as we look at it, even as we seek to understand it and to interpret it," Robert Handy confessed.[50] Sydney Ahlstrom stated a similar conviction even more frankly. "A new present has created a new past."[51] A significant volume published recently was entitled *Reinterpretation in American Church History.*[52]

Does this mean that historians have abandoned completely the work of their predecessors? Such an approach is neither desirable nor possible. It does mean, however, that their cherished presuppositions and traditional interpretations must be evaluated from different perspectives. Neither religious history in general nor Baptist history in particular can maintain a static existence.

Walter Rauschenbusch addressed a group of seminarians in 1914. "Today ministers do not have to be told that they must study the Bible, but they are, on the whole, as indifferent about history as Catholic priests used to be about Bible study."[53] The situation was little different in Morgan Edwards's day. Today the study of history and Bible study must be encouraged. "As I now see it," commented Sydney Mead, "the primary task of the historian of religion in America is to help members of the 'now' generation to see intellectually and accept emotionally the idea that clues to the nature of their true identity are to be found in the thoughts and actions of the 'then' generations that preceded them."[54] The first Baptist historian responded positively to major challenges and needs in his generation. With genuine insight, Edwards emphasized the

interrelatedness and lasting significance of Baptist history, denominational unity, and ministerial education. In the process, he provided Baptists with a lasting foundation for future historical endeavors.

Notes

1. "Theory and Practice in Historical Study: A Report of the Committee on
   Historiography" (New York: Social Science Research Council, Bulletin 54,
   1946), p. 134.
2. Ibid., p. 135.
3. Ibid.
4. Herbert Butterfield, *Man On His Past* (Cambridge: University Press, 1955),
   p. XIII.
5. Morgan Edwards, "A Farewell Discourse Delivered at the Baptist Meeting
   in Rye on Feb. 8, 1761" (Dublin, 1761), p. 17.
6. Funeral Address by William Rogers in John Rippon, *The Baptist Annual
   Register* (London: Messers Dilly, Button, and Thomas, n.d.), II, 313.
7. Ibid.
8. Ibid., p. 312.
9. David Spencer, *The Early Baptists of Philadelphia* (Philadelphia: William
   Syckelnoore, 1877), p. 91.
10. Cited by W. Morgan Patterson, "Our Baptist Heritage," *Baptist History
    and Heritage,* V (July, 1970), p. 131.
11. Albert C. Outler, "Theodosius' Horse: Reflections on the Predicament of
    the Church Historian," *Church History,* XXXIV (September, 1965), p.
    253.
12. Morgan Edwards, *Materials Towards A History of the Baptists in Pennsyl-
    vania* (Philadelphia: J. Crukshank and I. Collins, 1770).
13. A. D. Gillette, ed., *Minutes of the Philadelphia Baptist Association, from
    A.D. 1707, to A.D. 1807* (Philadelphia: American Baptist Publication
    Society, 1851), p. 85.
14. Rogers, p. 313.
15. Gillette, pp. 84-85.
16. Sidney E. Mead, "Church History Explained," *Church History,* XXXII
    (March, 1963), p. 18.
17. Ibid., p. 19.
18. Ibid.
19. Edwards, *The Baptists in Pennsylvania,* p. i.
20. Morgan Edwards, *Materials Towards A History of the Baptists in Jersey*
    (Philadelphia: T. Dobson, 1792), p. IV.

21. Ibid., p. V.
22. Edwards, *The Baptists in Pennsylvania*, p. ii.
23. Ibid., p. iii.
24. Morgan Edwards, "Materials for A History of the Baptists in Rhode Island," *Collections of the Rhode Island Historical Society*, VI (1867), 348.
25. Ibid., p. 304.
26. Ibid., p. 354.
27. Edwards, *The Baptists in Pennsylvania*, p. 48.
28. Rogers, p. 312.
29. See Reuben A. Guild, *Life, Times and Correspondence of James Manning, and the Early History of Brown University* (Boston: Gould and Lincoln, 1864), p. 44.
30. Gillette, pp. 128-129.
31. Guild, p. 45.
32. Rogers, p. 309.
33. Gillette, p. 87.
34. Morgan Edwards, "Materials Towards A History of the Baptists in South Carolina" (1772), p. 16.
35. Rogers, p. 310.
36. Edwards, *The Baptists in Jersey*, p. VI.
37. Ibid.
38. Morgan Edwards, "Materials Towards A History of the Baptists in Delaware State," *The Pennsylvania Magazine of History and Biography*, IX (1885), 213.
39. Cf. Isaac Backus, *A History of New England with Particular Reference to the Denomination of Christians Called Baptists* (2 vols., Newton, Mass.: Backus Historical Society, 1871).
40. Edwards, *The Baptists in Jersey*, p. V.
41. David Benedict, *Fifty Years Among the Baptists* (Glen Rose, Texas: Newman and Collings, n.d.), p. 23.
42. Edwards, *The Baptists in Jersey*, p. V.
43. Ibid.
44. Ibid., p. 151.
45. Morgan Edwards, *Two Academical Exercises on Subjects Bearing the Following Titles; Millennium, Last-Novelties* (Philadelphia: Dobson and Lang, 1788), pp. 5-6.
46. Rogers, p. 309.
47. Ibid.
48. Winthrop Hudson, "Shifting Trends in Church History" *Journal of Bible and Religion*, 28: 235-238, April, 1960.
49. See Jerald C. Brauer, ed., *Reinterpretation in American Church History* (Chicago: The University of Chicago Press, 1968), pp. 1-28.

50. Robert Handy, "Memories of the Future," *Foundations*, XIII (July-September, 1970), p. 198.
51. Sydney E. Ahlstrom, "The Problem of the History of Religion in America," *Church History*, XXXIX (June, 1970), p. 232.
52. Edited by Jerald C. Brauer.
53. Walter Rauschenbusch, "The Value and Use of History," *Foundations*, XII (July-September, 1969), p. 263.
54. Sidney Mead, "In Quest of America's Religion," *The Christian Century*, LXXXVII (June 17, 1970), p. 755.

2
English Baptist Response to the American Revolution

English Baptists at the outbreak of the American Revolution were in a period of "toleration and decline."[1] A rigid hyper-Calvinism virtually immobilized the Particular Baptist witness. General Baptists struggled against traditionalism and Socinianism. The tide was beginning to turn, however, partly as a result of indirect influence from the Wesleyan Awakening. Changing social conditions and the emergence of new leadership also contributed to the resurgence of religious vitality that persisted into the nineteenth century.

Outstanding leaders of Particular Baptists, especially in the Northampton Association, reflected concerns that climaxed in the evangelical theology of Andrew Fuller (1754-1815) and the missionary endeavors of William Carey (1761-1834). Dan Taylor (1738-1816), a Wesleyan convert who adopted Baptist views, led in forming the New Connection of General Baptists in 1770. The American Revolution, therefore, emerged at a time when English Baptists were involved in significant transitions. Many believed that the time had come for them to be fully recognized as English citizens with the right to participate freely in national life.

Introduction

Many English Baptists sympathized with the American colonies in their struggle for freedom. They joined with other Dissenters in petitioning repeatedly for the removal of civil and religious disabilities in England and regarded the American conflict as a fight for similar goals. "The Dissenters in general adopted the cause of the Americans and repudiated the measures of the Ministry as impolitic and unjust," asserted two historians of Dissent in 1808.[2] After the war, John Rippon (1750-1836), a prominent London pastor, declared:

I believe all our Baptist ministers in town, except two, and most of our brethern in the country, were on the side of the Americans in the late dispute ... We wept when the thirsty plains drank the blood of your departed heroes, and the shout of a king was amongst us when your well-fought battles were crowned with victory. And to this hour we believe that the independence of America will for a while secure the liberty of this country; but that if the continent had been reduced, Britain would not long have been free.[3]

Baptist leaders reflected little hesitancy in expressing their views. The younger Robert Hall (1764-1831) recalled the occasion during the war when his father, Robert Hall (1728-1791) of Arnesby accompanied him to Northampton to enroll in the boarding school conducted by John Collett Ryland (1723-1792). Ryland strongly favored the Americans, as did the elder Hall. The Northampton pastor declared in the course of the conversation that if he were General Washington he would call together his officers and have them bled into a punch bowl, himself the first. Then all should dip their swords in the bowl and solemnly swear not to sheathe them while an English soldier remained in America. Hall recalled his feelings at the time:

Only conceive, Sir, my situation, a poor little boy, that had never been out of his mother's chimney corner before, Sir, sitting by these two old gentlemen, and hearing this conversation about blood. Sir, I trembled at the idea of being left with such a bloody-minded master. Why, Sir, I began to think he would no more mind bleeding me, after my father was gone, than he would killing a fly. I quite expected to be bled, Sir.[4]

Rees David became pastor of St. Mary's, Norwich, in 1778 and from that time "fulminated against the American war. In two sermons preached and published in 1781 and 1782 he vindicated the colonists, condemned the British declaration of war on grounds both of principle and policy, and attacked the barbarity with which the war was being con-ducted abroad and the political corruption which supported it at home."[5]

English Baptists did not regard themselves as disloyal to their country in this matter. They believed that the welfare of the nation depended upon the abandoning of oppressive policies and the adoption of solutions mutually satisfactory to Englishmen and Americans. John Fawcett (1740-1817), pastor of the Wainsgate Church near Hebden Bridge, wrote John Sutcliffe (1752-1814) of Olney in 1775. "The affairs of this nation, I think, wear a gloomy aspect," he said. "Most who mention the unhappy contest with America here are desirous that lenient measures may be adopted, and that a speedy accommodation may take place."[6] A church in Suffolk reflected the same spirit in its minutes. "1776 January 16th. Appointed a solemn Fasting and Prayer for the state of the churches and the nation: that the Lord would appear for us and put a stop to the aboundings of sin and bring about a happy reconciliation between us and our colonies."[7] Years later, Robert Hall defended Dissenters against the charge of having involved the nation in the war: "It is well known they ever stood aloof from that scene of guilt and blood. Had their remonstrances been regarded, the calamities of that war had never been incurred."[8]

Modern historians concur in the assessment of English Baptist support for the Americans. "Nearly every Baptist saw that it was his cause at stake," observed the eminent British historian W. T. Whitley, "and while there was some caution to avoid trials for treason, the sympathy with the colonists was not always silent. It was not easy to fill the ranks of the British regiments," he continued, "and we do not know of a single Baptist there."[9] William McLoughlin reached a similar conclusion. "It seems from all the available evidence that the English Baptists were more thoroughly Whig than the Americans and lent their wholehearted support to the Revolutionary cause," he said. "In none of the extant letters from English Baptists is there a word about neutrality or about siding with the Crown."[10] McLoughlin did note that two English Baptist laymen encouraged American Baptist leaders to "act as neuters in the contest," but this appears to be an exceptional incident.[11]

The present study does not challenge the conclusion that English Baptists sympathized with and supported the Americans. The purpose of the study is rather to identify some of the principal spokesmen and to isolate some of the persistent themes in an effort to understand better Baptist involvements in the conflict. Some light should be thrown upon the Baptist rationale for active participation in political matters and upon the relation between religion and patriotism as understood by English Baptists in the late eighteenth century.

Principal Spokesmen

Few individuals influenced English Baptists in the eighteenth century more than Caleb Evans (1737-1791) of Bristol. Caleb studied under his father, Hugh Evans, and Bernard Foskett before enrolling in the dissenting academy at Mileend. While in London, he was baptized by Samuel Stennett of Little Wild Street. In 1759, Caleb accepted an invitation to assist his father at Broadmead, Bristol. About 1767, Caleb was ordained co-pastor of the church and served in the academy as well. The Bristol Education Society was formed under his leadership in 1770. "Under his fostering hand the most benevolent in all our connexions enrolled themselves as subscribers to the institution: and names, which add a lustre to any catalogue, became its patrons and benefactors," said John Rippon, one of several students destined to achieve prominence after studying under Evans.[12] King's College, Aberdeen, conferred on him the Doctor of Divinity degree in 1789.

Evans was drawn into political controversy by the publication of Wesley's *Calm Address.* The "grand question" for the latter was, "Has the English parliament power to tax the American colonies?"[13] Virtually without reservation, Wesley answered in the affirmative. Under the pseudonym Americanus, Evans responded for the other side *(Letter to the Rev. Mr. Wesley).* "He that is taxed without being represented, is a slave."[14]

The Bristol pastor accused Wesley of instability since a short time previously he had regarded the Americans an oppressed people, the policies of the ministry toward America as indefensible, and *An Argument in Defence of the Exclusive Right Claimed by the Colonies to Tax Themselves* a book that could be highly recommended. "The publication of Mr. Wesley's *Calm Address* occasioned a greater surprise than can easily be described amongst all ranks of people," he said.[15] An author identified as W. D. supplemented the arguments of Americanus, challenging Wesley's understanding of supreme power and the royal Charters.[16] Wesley was also accused of plagiarism by Evans and several others. "You present your Book to the world, as your own," asserted the author of *A Constitutional Answer,* "but the greatest part of it is taken *verbatim* from *Taxation No Tyranny,* written by the pensioned Dr. Johnson, a declared enemy of civil and religious liberty."[17]

In a second edition, Wesley admitted that Johnson's book had changed his mind on the matter of taxing the Americans. He had extracted the chief arguments, adding an application. But Wesley denied any knowledge of the book mentioned by Evans and asserted that the answer of Americanus was allegedly written by two Anabaptist ministers assisted by a Gentleman and a Tradesman of the Church of England. The Gentleman (James Rouquet) and Tradesman (William Pine) challenged these statements in letters to Wesley, who eventually recalled the circumstances. Believing that "a *public mistake* should be as publicly acknowledged and rectified,"[18] Evans finally published the pertinent materials in the *Gazeteer,* calling for a response. Wesley then publicly acknowledged the facts concerning his former opinions and the book in question essentially as described by Evans, after which the latter asserted that the matter was closed.[19]

Although personal aspects of the controversy with Wesley ended, the major question was unresolved. John Fletcher, Vicar of Madeley, Salop, published *A Vindication of the Rev. Mr. Wesley's Calm Address to Our American Colonies* in letters to Evans.[20] The vicar defended the conception of taxation maintained by Wesley as rational, scriptural, and constitutional: "Our sovereign, whether we have a vote for parliament men or not, has both a *right,* and a *power* to dispose, not only of our money, but also of our liberty and life."[21] The views of Evans were described as irrational, unscriptural, and unconstitutional. "If you are in the right," Fletcher said, "the sovereign is a tyrant, taxing the colonists is *robbery,* and enforcing such taxation by the sword is *murder.*"[22] Fletcher also appealed to the Bristol pastor as a protestant and a friend to liberty. In this connection, Evans was identified as a Calvinist and an Anabaptist, neither of which were highly regarded by the vicar of Madeley. In closing, Fletcher expressed the desire that by lenient measures toward the colonies "the government would bind them to their mother-country, both by the silken cords of pardoning love, and by the silver bands of some prerogatives, which may convince them, that Great Britain considers them, not only as subjects, but also as younger brothers."[23]

Evans responded quickly with *A Reply to the Rev. Mr. Fletcher's Vindication.* "I am therefore once more reluctantly drawn from the more pleasing and peaceful duties of my office as a minister of Christ, into the field of political controversy and am constrained, unequal as I feel myself to the important task, to plead in the best manner I am able, *pro patria.*"[24] The controversy with Wesley was reviewed before Evans focused upon the *Vindication.* Others had reported that the work was a worthy one, having been revised by Wesley and reviewed by Lord Dartmouth. "I confess, Sir, I was disappointed!—Instead of argument I met with nothing but declamation, instead of precision artful colouring, instead of proof presumption, instead of consistency contradiction, instead of reasoning a string of sophistries."[25]

Evans noted several apparent contradictions and dealt at length with the inseparability of taxation and representation. "Establish the *right* of another man to take from me *what he pleases,* and though he should actually take perhaps only a *shilling* in a year, I am a *slave,* I have *nothing* I can call *my own.*"[26] Representation might be unequal in England, yet it was present. "But who are the specific *virtual* representatives of *America?* Who are appointed to represent the property there?"[27] No one, reasoned Evans, thus to tax the Americans was unlawful.

Nor did Evans believe that such taxation was scriptural.

Should it be made to appear that the British parliament have authority from scripture, to tax their unrepresented brethren in *America,* and to cut their throats, burn their towns, and spread universal devastation amongst them because they do not chuse *(sic)* to submit to such taxation, it would furnish a stronger objection, in my opinion, against the divine original of the sacred code, than has ever yet been produced.[28]

If such were demonstrated, he would abide by the teaching of Scripture. Needless to say, however, Evans was not convinced that such was the case. He cited the Golden Rule as an example. "Now I presume the good people of England *would not be* willing that the Americans, in their assemblies, should tax *English property* here: And why should we therefore desire, in our parliament, to tax *American property* there?"[29]

The Bristol pastor declared his reverence for the British constitution, affirmed his loyalty to George III, and observed that he knew no king haters in England.

Your telling the world I am a Calvinist, and then giving your own horrid and fanciful description of Calvinism: and that I am an Anabaptist, and then presenting your readers with the most frightful picture of this sect is such a display of illiberality, meanness and impertinence, as would most exceedingly well have become a *Thomas Olivers,* but to which I should have thought a Mr. *Fletcher* must have been superior.[30]

In closing the reply, Evans also stated his desire for reconciliation and peace with the colonies.

From the purest motives, I most ardently desire and pray for the restoration of peace betwixt us and our colonies. And whether, addressing those who consider themselves the *injured* party, as *rebels,* and resisters of the *ordinance of God;*—or endeavoring to prevail upon those in power, to relax in their demands, to put on gentleness, to treat them with mildness, to reason with, rather than rail at and destroy them;—in short, to address them as *freemen,* and *younger brothers,* (to use your own words, *inconsistent* as they are from *your* pen,)—be the most *probably method* of restoring peace,—I submit to the decision of past experience, and the feelings of every generous mind.[31]

As might be expected, Fletcher responded. He wrote *American Patriotism Farther Confronted with Reason, Scripture, and the Constitution.* "Beasts and savages can be conquered by fire and sword," he said, "but it is the glory of men and Christians to be subdued by argument and scripture."[32] Evans characterized the work accurately as "dull repetition."[33] "The Americans are *protected,* and the British legislature is the *protecting* power," Fletcher declared. "The protected owe taxes to their protectors, and not the protectors to the protected."[34] He denied that ownership of property is absolute or that the origin of power is with the people. Evans had quoted several times from Richard Price *(Observations on the Nature of Civil Liberty),* and these statements were challenged at great length. Fletcher concluded with a scriptural plea for the revolted colonies and suggestions for effecting a reconciliation.

The exchange ended with Evans's *Political Sophistry Detected.* "The grand mistake of the *Anti-*American writers seems to me to be this," he said.

They suppose the King, Lords, and Commons, to be THE CONSTITUTION, whereas in fact they are only the *trustees,* the agents of the constitution; and should they therefore, be it by what combination of circumstances it will, *betray their trust,* instead of faithfully executing it, and we are no more bound to submit to them if we can avoid it, than we are to a highwayman who stops us on the road, if we have it in our power to withstand him.[35]

Evans described his politics as none other than those "of every Whig in the kingdom."[36] He was not seeking to undercut the British constitution but to defend, interpret, and apply it properly.[37] With Fletcher, he agreed that "arms . . . will never properly end the contest. Should we overpower the American colonies, they will remain unconvinced."[38] Fortunately, Evans lived to see the return of peace. On the hundreth anniversary of the Glorious Revolution (1788), he observed the occasion with a sermon entitled *British Freedom Realized.* "Perhaps no government under heaven, considering the imperfection of the present state, can be modelled upon a better plan than our own," he declared.[39] "Our divisions about the late unhappy war, concerning which the best of men entertained different ideas, are at an end," he said, "and blessed be God we are once more, and what good man but must exult in it, an united and happy people."[40]

The General Baptist pastor Joshua Toulmin (1740-1815) likewise expressed himself in print at an early stage of the American Revolution. Toulmin was born in London and educated under Calvinist teachers, whose views he rejected. After serving as pastor of a Presbyterian church for a brief time, Toulmin adopted Baptist views. In 1765, he became the pastor of the General Baptist Chapel in Taunton, remaining there for thirty-eight years. Along with many other General Baptists, Toulmin was influenced by Socinianism. He published a biography of Socinius in 1777. For his new and expanded edition of Daniel Neal's *History of the Puritans,* Harvard College conferred upon him the Doctor of Divinity degree (1794). *The American War Lamented: A Sermon Preached at Taunton, February the 18th. and 25th., 1776* expressed his views concerning the Revolution.[41]

Toulmin considered the cause and motives of war, its dreadful effects and possible consequences, and war as a judgment of God. Attributing the cause of war to the lusts of power and conquest, the Baptist pastor painted the dreadful effects in graphic terms. As possible consequences, he described the uncertainty of the outcome and peculiar evils by which "whoever gains a victory, victory itself is to be feared and lamented."[42] In retrospect, the uncertainty depicted by Toulmin appears prophetic.

Many unforeseen accidents happen to frustrate the wisest schemes and best concerted measures, especially in operations that depend upon the leave of the winds and waves to execute, as well as where the ground is preoccupied; where we oppose those who fight in the sight of their houses, their families, and children; where our forces are not inured to the climate, or may be unacquainted with the situation.[43]

Distrust of the wisdom of the Cabinet and former defeats at the hands of the Americans were other factors noted. The Baptist pastor left little doubt about where his sympathies lay.

The unanimity and firmness of our Colonies, whom one judgment unites, and one spirit actuates; the ENTHUSIASM which warms their breasts, the ardour with which all glow in one common cause; these are circumstances very unfavorable to the success of those whom different judgments, on the merit of the cause, divide; who are, perhaps, reluctant to the service of the field, and who are not animated with the *enthusiasm* a contest for freedom inspires. Let these things be weighed, and it will at least appear a matter of doubt, whether the event will be so propitious to the *British* arms as some expect.[44]

Regardless of the military outcome, Toulmin was convinced that victory was impossible for the British. If the colonies were subdued, their economic contributions would be nullified and their political loyalty further reduced. The independence of the colonies, a loss of trade, and probably war with England's natural enemies could result from a victory by the Americans.

Toulmin expounded at length upon war as a judgment of God. By war, divine Providence recovers nations or ruins nations. "On what grounds can we look up to him, whilst the cloud is gathering and ready to burst upon us?" he inquired. "On what grounds can we hope that Heaven hath kind designs toward us?"[45] His answer was not very encouraging. The British could not plead their piety, regularity, and sobriety of public manners, national virtue, or innocence. "Let us pray to the God of heaven, to forgive us our sins, to avert the impending storm, and to restore peace and good-will to all parts of our empire."[46]

Toulmin quoted extensively from Richard Price, who portrayed the colonists in idealistic terms and censured the British for their many vices. "Yes, my brethren, the mercy of heaven, published by Jesus Christ, indulges those with liberty to hope, who have no merit to plead, but even much guilt to confess."[47] With this hope in mind, and in the context of prayer, Toulmin articulated his desire for dealing with the situation at hand.

Let us intreat the Lord of Lords, and King of Kings, that our most gracious sovereign may, from the clemency of his disposition, interpose to stop the further effusion of human blood, by forming and directing pacific measures— measures that may prevent the devastations of war, and re-unite all the members of this great empire in the sacred bond of charity, harmony and public happiness.[48]

Not all Baptists agreed with the views cited thus far. John Martin (1741-1820) represents one notable exception. Martin became pastor of the Grafton Street Chapel, London, in 1773, and remained there until his death. A staunch Calvinist and political conservative, he resisted Fullerism, as well as the American and French Revolutions. "When he lifted up his feet," said Fuller, "he was always careful to put them down again in the same place."[49] Martin created widespread concern by charging during the French Revolution that many Dissenters would join the French if they invaded England. Late in the century the Grafton Street pastor administered the *Regium Donum* and defended the Test and Corporation Acts.

Martin commented upon the American Revolution in *Familiar Dialogues Between Americus and Britannicus* (1776). King and parliament might err, making and executing oppressive acts. But "who are to judge whether any act which has the genuine stamp of legal authority, be unwise, oppressive or unjust?"[50] For the individual to judge such matters would be chaos. Thus, "it is the duty of persons who are *voluntarily* connected together in civil society, to submit to the leading members of that society whenever they are joined by a respectable majority of the whole."[51]

Britannicus (Martin) restricted the right of private judgment and defended passive obedience and nonresistance.

For my part, I am fully convinced, that government and governors are from above, and ordained for our advantage. The persons however, who reap the greatest advantage from the government under which they reside, are those who are willingly, practically and conscientiously subject to its just demands: And what are its just demands is not always in the power of every individual to determine.[52]

The views of Caleb Evans received some attention in Martin's *Dialogues,* but the views of Richard Price were criticized at great length. "What does the *Doctor* mean by liberty? Why, that every *fop* and every *fool,* as well as every wise and prudent man, should be guided by his own will, or be under the direction of self-government; for whatever affects that, in the *Doctor's* opinion, introduces slavery."[53] Martin challenged this concept of free will, citing Jonathan Edwards as a major authority. If government originates with the people and is conducted under their direction, the fasting and prayer recommended by Price is meaningless. Further, the partisan description of religious conditions in England and America was considered unjust. At this point, Martin expounded at length upon the treatment of the Indians by Americans and questioned whether they were as righteous as Price contended.

Price also asserted that the Americans were seeking a better constitution and more liberty. If their goal was independence, argued Britannicus, why did they regard themselves as loyal subjects seeking adequate representation. Taxation and representation should no longer be mentioned. "I had much rather the revolting colonists were abandoned, and left to lament at leisure their own folly," Martin observed in closing, "than to hear of their being drenched in blood."[54] Martin doubted, however, that hostilities would soon cease. "If the ties of *interest, honour* and *affection,* will not bind us to each other, every other effort will be in vain."[55]

One of the most avid supporters of the colonists during the revolution was Robert Robinson (1735-1790) of Cambridge. Converted under the preaching of George Whitefield, Robinson became a Baptist in 1759. A small congregation in Cambridge soon sought his services as pastor, and Robinson remained there until his death. Under his ministry, the congregation increased in numbers, resources, and influence. The Cambridge pastor established himself among the Protestant Dissenters as an eloquent preacher, capable scholar, and champion of liberty. "With the events, that passed from the period at which Great Britain first formed the determination of framing laws for America, till that when the United States of America rendered themselves independent," said his friend and biographer George Dyer, "he had a most accurate acquaintance."[56] After the war "very handsome proposals were made him, to settle in the United States: and in the joy experienced by the Americans, on having established their independence, he most cordially anticipated."[57]

With the publication of *Arcana* (1774),[58] requesting relief for Dissenters in the matter of subscription, Robinson identified himself as a profound spokesman for freedom. "When I was told that the *Arcana* was written by a Baptist minister, I replied, no, it cannot be: we have not one amongst us who can write such a book," said Daniel Turner of Abingdon.[59]

During the war (1780), Robinson preached a sermon from Romans 13 entitled "Christian Submission to Civil Government." Paul was speaking of government, not governors, he argued. Further, Paul was speaking of good civil government that would protect life, liberty, property, conscience, and justice. Thus, Paul meant to exhort Christians never to resist but always to support *good* civil government. "God forbid we should think St. Paul an enemy to civil and religious liberty."[60]

A Political Catechism was written near the close of the war (1782). In a later advertisement, Robinson commented:

During the administration that prosecuted the unhappy war with America, all who had the virtue and courage to avow sound principles of civil government, were reproached with want of loyalty to the crown, and respect for government, and the struggles of liberty were called by many an ignoble soul, inflammatory, republican, and seditious.[61]

The *Catechism* was designed to aid in disseminating safe political principles. It emphasized government by the people on the basis of a compact, defined good civil government along the lines previously mentioned, and defended the right of resistance. "There is a line beyond which the people cannot bear oppression, and that right to call rulers to account was always understood to belong to the people."[62] Concerning the Americans, Robinson said: "It will be entirely their own fault if they do not frame the largest and most free empire in the world. Let trade, and not dominion, be their object, and they have duration and glory before them."[63]

Persistent Themes

Samuel Stennett (1728-1795) of Little Wild Street, London, was one of the more moderate and conciliatory Baptist leaders during the Revolutionary period. Educated and sophisticated, he represented Baptists and other Dissenters in contacts with notable political and ecclesiastical figures. Upon occasion, he intervened in behalf of Baptists seeking relief in America. His American correspondence reflects a genuine interest in religious developments in the new world.

A decade after the close of the war (1793), Stennett published *A Trip to Holyhead*, describing conversations between a Churchman and a Dissenter as they traveled in a mail coach and discussed issues of the day. Topics of concern were the Toleration Act (1688), the extension of that act (1779), the American War, the question of reform, possible repeal of the Test and Corporation Acts, and the French Revolution.[64]

Stennett set forth several major themes which have particular pertinence to this study and are reflected in numerous other Baptist and Dissenting works. "Dissenters are, and ever must be, if they act consistently with their principles and interest, Whigs," he declared. They were described as friends of the British constitution and strong defenders of the revolution in 1688. "That is the glorious era whence they date their liberties."[65]

As a consequence, Dissenters defended the right of resistance, opposing concepts of passive obedience and nonresistance. Even John Martin did not deny that under some circumstances resistance was necessary. The issue, therefore, was whether circumstances justified resistance by the Americans. Dissenters had demonstrated their loyalty to the Hanover succession and regarded the king as a protector of their liberties. They would not support any effort to overthrow the monarchy.

Another point was emphasized by Stennett. "Dissenters, take them as a body, have not been accustomed to meddle with politics. The generality of them through the kingdom are plain pious people, whose minds are more occupied with the concerns of another world than this."[66] Dissenters seldom discussed politics in their gatherings, except when apprehensive about being deprived of their religious liberties. The same was true of their ministers, who had "more important matters to attend to than questions of policy and jurisprudence, which fall to the department of the court and the senate."[67] Richard Price and Joseph Priestly were exceptions and had done "a great deal of good and a great deal of harm."[68] These men were not popular among the masses of Dissenters.

The American war had originated in "a concurrence of circumstances," none of which the Dissenters had initiated.[69] George III created uneasiness by dismissing a Whig ministry. Rumors then circulated that a change of principles had taken place, and the rumors were circulated in the colonies. Mutual confidence declined, to which governors in the northern colonies contributed by sending home alarming reports of possible rebellion. "They were, however, still on both sides reluctant to a separation, insomuch that neither party could persuade itself, that the opposite meant to push things to extremities. This is well known to have been a fact as to the Americans."[70] The colonists were finally convinced that chains were being forged by a despotic Tory ministry, and they "began to form, unite, and prepare for resistance."[71]

Finally Stennett, along with many others, stressed the providence of God as operative in what had taken place. "The vast variety of circumstances which contributed to the loss of the Colonies, operated, as is the case in all events, especially those of such magnitude, under the direction and control of divine Providence," he said. "This calamity, taken in the whole round of it, was meant, no doubt, to chastise both their and our national ingratitude, and other crying vices."[72]

Conclusion

Correspondence between Baptist leaders in England and America continued until the outbreak of hostilities and resumed as soon as the war ended. Some English Baptist ministers preached and wrote concerning the war, and most expressed encouragement and support for the Americans. An abridgment or extension of liberty in America was considered influential upon the struggle for liberty in England. The fight for freedom combined the talents of General and Particular Baptists, evangelical Christians, and Rational Dissenters. Virtually all agreed that the supreme power in government was lodged in the people, who must judge concerning its integrity and effectiveness, seeking redress when government became unduly oppressive. John Locke was their great authority. But they also stressed the guiding hand of Providence and felt "disposed to place firm confidence in the great Governor of the world, and to address their ardent prayers to him that *his kingdom may come, and his will be done on earth as it is in heaven.*"[73]

Notes

1. A. C. Underwood, *A History of the English Baptists* (London: The Carey Kingsgate Press Limited, 1956), p. 116.

2. Bogue and Bennett, cited by Anthony Lincoln, *Some Political and Social Ideas of English Dissent 1763-1800* (Cambridge: University Press, 1938), p. 25.

3. Reuben Aldridge Guild, *Life, Times, and Correspondence of James Manning and the Early History of Brown University* (Boston: Gould and Lincoln, 1864), p. 324.

4. Cited by H. Wheeler Robinson, *The Life and Faith of the Baptists* (London: The Kingsgate Press, 1946), p. 65.

5. Charles Boardman Jewson, *The Baptists in Norfolk* (London: The Carey Kingsgate Press Limited, 1957), p. 55.

6. Letter, John Fawcett to John Sutcliffe, 1775.

7. Ashley J. Klaiber, *The Story of the Suffolk Baptists* (London: The Kingsgate Press, 1931), p. 107.

8. John Foster, *Miscellaneous Works and Remains of the Rev. Robert Hall* (London: Henry G. Bohn, 1846), p. 215.

9. W. T. Whitley, *A History of the British Baptists* (London: Charles Griffin and Company, Limited, 1923), p. 234.

10. William G. McLoughlin, *New England Dissent 1630-1833* (2 vols.; Cambridge, Massachusetts: Howard University Press, 1971), I, 582.

11. Ibid., p. 583.

12. John Rippon, ed., *The Baptist Annual Register* (4 vols.; 1790-1802), III, 442.

13. John Wesley, *A Calm Address to Our American Colonies* (London: Printed by R. Hawes, 1775), p. VII.

14. Caleb Evans, *Letter to the Rev. Mr. Wesley, Occasioned by his Calm Address to Our American Colonies, 1775.*

15. Caleb Evans, *A Reply to the Rev. Mr. Fletcher's Vindication of Mr. Wesley's Calm Address to Our American Colonies* (Bristol: Printed and sold by W. Pine, 1775), p. 4.

16. W. D., *A Second Answer to Mr. John Wesley. Being A Supplement to the Letter of Americanus* (London: Printed for Wallis and Stonehouse, 1775).

17. *A Constitutional Answer to the Rev. Mr. John Wesley's Calm Address to the American Colonies* (London: Printed for E. and C. Dilly, 1775), p. 3.

18. Evans, *A Reply to the Rev. Mr. Fletcher's Vindication*, p. 15.

19. Ibid., p. 19.

20. John Fletcher, *A Vindication of the Rev. Mr. Wesley's Calm Address to Our American Colonies* (Second edition corrected; London: Printed by R. Hawes, 1776).

21. Ibid., p. 8.

22. Ibid., p. 7.

23. Ibid., p. 70.

24. Evans, *A Reply to the Rev. Mr. Fletcher's Vindication*, p. 3.

25. Ibid., p. 24.

26. Ibid., p. 36.

27. Ibid., p. 37.

28. Ibid., p. 51.

29. Ibid., p. 52.

30. Ibid., p. 84. Olivers had published *A Full Defense of the Rev. John Wesley, in Answer to the Several Personal Reflections Cast on that Gentleman by the Rev. Caleb Evans.*

31. Ibid., p. 89.

32. J. Fletcher, *American Patriotism* (Second edition; London: printed by R. Hawes, 1777), p. V.

33. Caleb Evans, *Political Sophistry Detected, or, Brief Remarks on the Rev. Mr. Fletcher's Late Tract, Entitled American Patriotism* (Bristol: W. Pine, 1776), p. 4.

34. Fletcher, *American Patriotism*, p. 12.

35. Evans, *Political Sophistry Detected*, pp. 14-15.

36. Ibid., p. 15.

37. See Caleb Evans, *British Constitutional Liberty* (Published 1775).

38. Evans, *Political Sophistry Detected*, p. 36.

39. Caleb Evans, *British Freedom Realized* (Bristol: W. Pine, 1788), p. 22.

40. Ibid., pp. 28-29.

41. Joshua Toulmin, *The American War Lamented* (London: Printed for J. Johnson, 1776).

42. Ibid., p. 3.

43. Ibid., p. 9.

44. Ibid., p. 10.

45. Ibid., p. 13.
46. Ibid., p. 17.
47. Ibid., p. 18.
48. Ibid., p. 19.
49. Underwood, p. 164.
50. John Martin, *Familiar Dialogues Between Americus and Britannicus* (London: printed for J. Wilkie, 1776), p. 12.
51. Ibid., p. 20.
52. Ibid., p. 33.
53. Ibid., pp. 52-53.
54. Ibid., p. 74.
55. Ibid.
56. George Dyer, *Memoirs of the Life and Writings of Robert Robinson* (London: Printed for G. G. and J. Robinson, 1796), p. 121.
57. Ibid., p. 122.
58. See *Miscellaneous Works of Robert Robinson*, 4 Vols. (Harlow: printed by B. Flower, 1807).
59. Graham W. Hughes, *With Freedom Fired: The Story of Robert Robinson Cambridge Nonconformist* (London: The Carey Kingsgate Press Limited, 1955), p. 44.
60. Robinson, *Miscellaneous Works,* III, 291.
61. Ibid., II, 259.
62. Ibid., p. 328.
63. Ibid., p. 355.
64. Samuel Stennett, *A Trip to Holyhead* in William Jones, ed., *The Works of Samuel Stennett,* D.D., 3 Vols. (London: Printed for Thomas Tegg, 1824), III, 461-524.
65. Ibid., pp. 476-477.
66. Ibid., p. 478.
67. Ibid.
68. Ibid., p. 479.
69. Ibid., p. 480.
70. Ibid.
71. Ibid.
72. Ibid., p. 483.
73. Ibid., pp. 517-518.

3
Significance of the Formation
of the Triennial Convention

Seven North American Baptist denominations cooperated for several years (1959-1964) in the Baptist Jubilee Advance movement. At a historic gathering in Atlantic City, New Jersey, during May, 1964, representatives from the participating groups provided a fitting climax for the movement by jointly celebrating the sesquicentennial anniversary of the formation of the Triennial Convention. In this and many other ways, Baptists throughout the United States and Canada have acknowledged a common heritage in their first national organization. The purpose of this chapter is to discuss some specific areas in which the formation of the Triennial Convention has been significant for Baptists in North America.

Significance for Baptist Organization

No organization above the local church level appeared among American Baptists during the seventeenth century. The few existing fellowships simply struggled for survival. But five churches constituted the Philadelphia Association in 1707, thereby advancing organizational development to a second level. Calvinistic in theology and progressive in spirit, this association within about half a century increased fivefold and encompassed churches from New York to Virginia.

Forty-four years elapsed between the founding of the first and second associations. Resulting in part from religious persecution, theological divisions, numerical weakness, geographical dispersion, untrained leadership, and individualistic attitudes, this gradual associational development proved to be more of an asset than a liability. During these years the Philadelphia Association evolved, by trial and error, a rather structured system of organization and practice which served as the model for a complex of associations which emerged rapidly during the last half of the eighteenth century.

Associations among Baptists increased to forty-eight before 1800. Advisory councils formed voluntarily by representatives from local churches; they disclaimed all coercive authority except the right to withdraw fellowship from individuals or churches that deviated from accepted doctrine and practice. But these autonomous associations composed of autonomous churches maintained a remarkable denominational solidarity primarily because they adhered closely to the pattern of organization and procedure developed at Philadelphia. Leadership and literature produced by this parent association perpetuated its traditions. Sister associations imitated the Philadelphia example by aiding weak and destitute churches, exercising discipline, answering queries, supporting itinerant missionaries, maintaining associational funds, and dispatching annual circular letters. The various associations also exchanged messengers and correspondence, encouraged publications designed to extend and defend Baptist principles, and cooperated in the fight for freedom. Thus, as the eighteenth century ended, Baptists in America constituted one denominational fellowship united on basic principles and approaches, but they were not united into one general organization.

The process of assimilating divergent elements of Baptist life into a denominational unity apart from some organizational structure became increasingly difficult as the nineteenth century progressed. The rapid numerical expansion continued. By 1812, the Baptist constituency included 172,972 members, 2,164 churches, and 112 associations. Conceivably, various forces could have led these scattered individuals and organizations in several directions. Besides, beginning in 1802, a number of domestic missionary societies came into existence among Baptists. Basing membership upon financial contributions alone, these societies functioned as practical organizations through which interested individuals could channel their missionary efforts and contributions. Created and promoted almost without exception by Baptist associations, these societies operated without conscious hostility toward the older organizations. But they also operated without coordinating their activities with those of other societies and associations.

The appalling need for a general organization among Baptists became apparent when Luther Rice returned to America in 1813 and sought support for the foreign mission enterprise. An inspired constituency responded by appointing delegates who convened at Philadelphia during May, 1814, and organized "The General Missionary Convention of the Baptist Denomination in the United States of America, for Foreign Missions." Against the background sketched previously, several comments may be made concerning the significance of this event for Baptist organization.

First, the Triennial Convention represented the first national organization. Delegates from eleven states and the District of Columbia participated in its formation. Considered "the elite of the Denomination,"[1] the group was regarded by contemporaries as "large and propitious."[2] These delegates formulated "a plan for eliciting, combining, and directing the Energies of *the whole Denomination* in one sacred effort."[3] Some denominational fragmentation occurred later as individuals opposed the work of the convention, but all appearances indicate that a more radical fragmentation would have occurred without the existence of this general organization and its appealing purpose. The Triennial Convention aided the cause of national Baptist unity at a crucial time.

Second, the formation of the convention accelerated the society development among the local Baptist groups. Even before Rice returned from India, Boston Baptists organized a foreign mission society. A committee appointed for the purpose reported on seventeen such societies to the delegates who gathered for the historic meeting in Philadelphia. Luther Rice had aided personally in organizing many of these bodies as he toured the nation seeking support for the foreign mission enterprise. Recognizing the usefulness of the procedure, the convention appointed Rice as its missionary and instructed him

to continue his itinerant services, in these United States, for a reasonable time; with a view to excite the public mind more generally, to engage in Missionary exertions; and to assist in originating Societies, or Institutions, for carrying the Missionary design into execution.[4]

For several years the number of societies doubled annually. As Baptists' interests expanded, they formed benevolent societies for other than missionary purposes. Within a reasonable length of time, societies became an accepted part of Baptist organizational life.

Since Christian groups at that time, almost without exception, used societies for promoting benevolent causes, particularly missions, this development among Baptists in America should not be considered abnormal. Yet many individuals realized that societies failed to provide a satisfactory denominational structure because of their restricted purposes and their tenuous connection with the churches. Consequently, the Triennial Convention leaders began to advocate that representatives from the various associations form state conventions, which in turn could select delegates for a general convention. Efforts to transform the existing convention into such an organization, climaxing with the "Great Reversal" of 1826, proved abortive. However, unifying tendencies stimulated and encouraged by the Triennial Convention hastened the formation of state conventions. Beginning with South Carolina in 1821, sixteen groups organized state conventions in slightly more than a decade. Although violently opposed in some areas, these conventions gradually attracted the larger Baptist constituency. In many cases where the activities of area missionary societies overlapped with those of the state conventions, the involved organizations merged. As might be expected, the structure of the resulting bodies varied widely. Thus, the formation of the Triennial Convention influenced Baptist organization in a third area by hastening the formation and affecting the character of state conventions.

Finally, the formation of the Triennial Convention conditioned Baptists for national rather than for sectional planning. With reference to Baptist organization, this prepared the way for other national societies, particularly the Baptist General Tract Society (1824); the American Baptist Home Mission Society (1832); and the American and Foreign Bible Society (1837). Supported and administered by the same national constituency, these independent entities usually coordinated their activities and meetings with those of the Triennial Convention. The slavery issue injected a sectional spirit into Baptist life that in 1845 produced division, but a national outlook lingered. Adapting the Triennial Convention constitution for use by the Southern Baptist Convention, delegates at Augusta proposed to unite "such portions of the Baptist denomination *in the United States,* as may desire a general organization for Christian benevolence, which shall fully respect the independence and equal rights of the Churches."[5] In an address to the public, they affirmed, "The Constitution we adopt is precisely that of the original union.... We recede from it no single step."[6] Baptists of the North abandoned the Triennial Convention constitution entirely. They formed as its successor the "American Baptist Missionary Union." Since that time, several major Baptist fellowships have arisen; but all of them possess a common heritage in the Triennial Convention.

Significance for Baptist Expansion

Events surrounding the formation of the Triennial Convention launched the Baptists of America into the foreign mission enterprise. "Up to this time," said Benedict, "this large and increasing body seemed to have had no idea that they had either the call or the ability to send out missionaries to foreign lands."[7] Admittedly, they were interested in such efforts and supported the ventures of others. But they needed "some general excitement" so that "the means within their power might be called into action."[8] The conversion of Luther Rice and Adoniram Judson to Baptist views provided the necessary stimulus.

The delegates who convened in Philadelphia remedied the immediate situation that had inspired the assembly by appointing Judson and Rice as missionaries. But they projected a program of world missions that reached far beyond these appointments. "What advantages soever particular fields for missionary efforts may exhibit," stated their address to the public, "the disciple of Jesus will contemplate the whole world as a scene demanding his sympathy and his prayers, his zeal and his contributions."[9]

The convention constitution assigned the responsibility for administering the world missions program to a Board of Commissioners. But the assembled delegates recognized also that financial support and missionary personnel must come from the larger constituency. They pleaded, therefore, for "zealous cooperation" from the total denomination, citing as motivating factors:

the brevity of life, the value of immortal souls, the obligations under which divine mercy has laid us, our past inactivity, the facility with which the great work may be effected, the excellent tendency of the spirit for foreign Missions in multiplying Missions at home, the examples of other christian *(sic)* persuasions, and the incalculable blessings that may follow our endeavours.[10]

The constituency responded enthusiastically. Within a year the Board of Commissioners was enabled to commission new appointees. Instructions delivered to these individuals reflect the extensive influence that English Baptist missionary procedures exerted upon the Board's policies during the formative years. Urging the missionaries to maintain high standards of conduct, avoid political entanglements, and master the native language, the Board also instructed them to engage in translation work, establish schools and a church, and communicate frequently with the homeland. An emphasis upon cooperation with and imitation of the Serampore mission under William Carey pervaded the instructions.[11] In time, the Board refined its policies, increased its personnel, expanded its areas of operation, and finally dissolved. But its several successors have retained a commitment to world missions that began with the "morning hour" when Baptists of America united in the General Missionary Convention.

Regarding foreign missions as "in reality only domestic missions extended,"[12] Baptist leaders demonstrated genuine insight by recognizing the mutual dependence of each upon the other. And for a brief period (1817-1826), the Triennial Convention engaged in both enterprises. But, except for Indian missions, the domestic activities of the convention lacked popular support. Nevertheless, the formation of the Triennial Convention generated a domestic missionary spirit that greatly aided Baptist expansion in America.

Robert Semple attended the first convention as a delegate of the Richmond Society. At the Potomac River, a small Baptist group intercepted him and requested "ministerial help," which they afterward received. Since "Rice's travels and exertions had produced pretty generally among Virginia Baptists a missionary spirit, little difficulty was found in obtaining the sanction of the Richmond Society or in procuring the necessary funds," Semple reported.[13]

This incident illustrates several typical features of the expanding home mission enterprise. First, exertions on behalf of foreign missions created a congenial atmosphere for productive home mission efforts. In

1815, the Baptist Board reported that attention to foreign missions had "revived the spirit of domestic missions, and even originated, or excited, a regard to this subject in places where, before, it either did not exist, or was totally inactive."[14] Also, publicity that circulated concerning the organization of local societies and a national convention stimulated requests for assistance by isolated Baptist groups. Moreover, the societies which emerged usually supported both foreign and home missions, almost always retaining a substantial portion of the funds collected for local uses. Quickly, therefore, the denomination developed a greater sensitivity regarding the responsibility of Christians for proclaiming the gospel at home, as well as abroad. Although complex circumstances forced the Triennial Convention from permanent participation in the enterprise, loyal convention supporters in 1832 organized the American Baptist Home Mission Society. Preparation that insured the success of this venture began with the formation of the Triennial Convention.

Significance for Baptist Education

Baptist churches in America from the beginning avoided specific educational prerequisites in ordaining ministerial candidates. At times, many appeared indifferent or even hostile to an educated ministry. Persecution during the Colonial period by a learned clergy intensified this prejudice, particularly in New England and the South; but Baptist leaders in the Middle Colonies fostered several educational ventures that partially transformed these negative attitudes toward learning. As early as 1722, the Philadelphia Association endeavored without success to secure for potential Baptist ministers four scholarships which Thomas Hollis, a wealthy English Baptist, had established at Harvard College. Ministerial candidates in the association studied under private tutors and attended institutions which other denominations had established.

Isaac Eaton inaugurated a new educational era for Baptists in 1756 by founding a Latin Grammar School at Hopewell, New Jersey. Ministers trained in this school and elsewhere diffused a healthy respect for education which aided the successful founding of Rhode Island College in 1764. Many associations supported the new college, established educational funds to assist worthy candidates, and encouraged local pastors in founding several academies. Because of these efforts, Baptists in America continued to respect and promote education, but rapid expansion on the frontier militated against significantly elevating the educational level of the ministry.

The first education society among American Baptists appeared only two years before the Triennial Convention was formed. But after the latter event, the number of such societies multiplied, a general concern for ministerial training increased, and several educational institutions were established. The major factors influencing this development arose in connection with convention activities and emphases.

Participation in the common missionary endeavor by trained and untrained ministers often produced mutual respect where prejudice had existed. Also, the need for missionary personnel intensified demands for an educated ministry. Further, the convention provided a forum where interested leaders could discuss the educational cause before an influential group. And finally, convention leaders and literature promoted this concern at local levels and for a time supported a national institution.

The first national assembly expressed a genuine interest in ministerial education: "While we avow our belief that a refined or liberal education is not an indispensible qualification for ministerial service, let us never lose sight of its real importance, but labour to help our young men by our contributions, by the origination of education Societies, and if possible, by a general theological seminary."[15] At the 1817 meeting, the venerated president, Richard Furman, outlined a systematic plan for supporting ministerial training. The convention included the cause of education in its constitution at that time. "The difficulties on this subject felt by some pious brethren," the delegates opined, "are, like vapours of the morning, vanishing."[16]

The convention delegated the Baptist Board with the responsibility for giving the president's plan "maturity and publicity" but expressed hope that some educational venture might be "speedily and vigorously attempted."[17] Spearheaded by the enthusiasm of Luther Rice, the Board acted more speedily and vigorously than some individuals desired in founding Columbian College at Washington, D.C. Divided into classical and theological departments, the institution received national support for several years. But interest subsided as financial difficulties increased, and in 1826 the convention dissociated itself from the college. From that time various individuals, educational societies, and state conventions intensified their efforts in behalf of local institutions. Within a few years many states contained at least one Baptist school. This pattern of educational support at the state level has continued, particularly in the South, although theological seminaries are currently supported by a broader constituency.

Significance for Baptist Identity

The delegates that formed the Triennial Convention regarded the action as divinely inspired. They were convinced that God had been instrumental in changing the baptismal sentiments of Judson and Rice in order to arouse a concern for foreign missions among Baptists. President Furman reflected the collective mind when he declared, "At the call of Divine Providence we are here assembled."[18] The convention received immediate, enthusiastic support mostly because this conviction had permeated the larger constituency. Thus an intensified consciousness of divine leadership and approval undergirded denominational activities that followed.

A deepened conviction concerning personal responsibility emerged among Baptists. "Assurances of divine assistance were never designed to discourage human endeavours,"[19] they said. As never before, individual Baptists became stewardship conscious. Male and female, young and old, rich and poor, black and white, they organized, contributed, prayed, and worked for the missionary enterprise. Several additional concerns such as Sunday School promotion, Bible and tract distribution, publication ventures, and other benevolent projects also engaged their attention. These endeavors demonstrated the progressive spirit that existed among Baptists after the formation of the convention, although the total impetus for their rise and spread obviously could not be attributed to this event. However, the national body reflected a favorable attitude toward such programs, promoted specific enterprises wherever possible, and produced a conducive atmosphere where progressive developments could transpire as individuals cooperated with God in accomplishing his purposes.

The first national assembly reminded Baptists that voluntary cooperation depended upon mutual acquaintance and confidence. Realizing that only voluntary cooperation could capitalize upon the many "important advantages" inherent in united efforts while protecting the independence of the churches, the delegates expressed a desire for an improved denominational fellowship where voluntarism could survive. "Is it not a fact that our churches are ignorant of each other to a lamentable degree?" they declared.[20] The travels of Luther Rice, information disseminated by the convention, organizational meetings, and participation in common enterprises gradually brought Baptists from different areas and backgrounds closer together. This process began at Philadelphia when "the sight of brethren who had never met each other before, and who a few months ago had never expected to meet on earth, afforded mutual and unutterable pleasure." They felt as though "the first interviews of heaven had been anticipated."[21]

Finally, the formation of the Triennial Convention has provided Baptists with a continuing source of inspiration and challenge. The Baptist Jubilee Advance movement, for example, informed the denominational family about this common heritage. But the movement also promoted fellowship among the participating groups, inspiring them to project programs designed to perpetuate the principles and spirit that undergirded the Triennial Convention. The North American Baptist Fellowship formed in 1966 remains as a visible organization committed to these purposes. Bold Mission Thrust of the Southern Baptist Convention indicates that the missionary spirit still prevails. Future Baptists will realize the significant results produced by these efforts, which demonstrate the spiritual dynamic that has emanated until the present from the formation of the first national organization.

Notes

1. William Bullein Johnson, "Reminiscences," in Hortense Woodson, *Giant in the Land* (Nashville, Tennessee: Broadman Press, 1950), pp. 33-34.
2. *The Baptist Memorial and Monthly Chronicle,* June, 1842, p. 192.
3. *Proceedings of the Baptist Convention for Missionary Purposes,* 1814, p. 3 (italics inserted).

4. Ibid., p. 13.
5. *Proceedings of the Southern Baptist Convention,* 1845, p. 3 (italics inserted).
6. Ibid., p. 19.
7. David Benedict, *Fifty Years Among the Baptists* (New York: Sheldon and Company, 1860), p. 112.
8. Letter from Lucius Bolles to Luther Rice, December 7, 1813, in James B. Taylor, *Memoir of Rev. Luther Rice,* Second edition (Nashville, Tennessee: Broadman Press, 1937), p. 134.
9. *Proceedings of the Baptist Convention for Missionary Purposes,* 1814, p. 40.
10. Ibid., p. 41.
11. See *The Second Annual Report of the Baptist Board of Foreign Missions for the United States,* 1816, pp. 113-116.
12. *The First Annual Report of the Baptist Board of Foreign Missions for the United States,* 1815, p. 6.
13. Cited by Garnett Ryland, *The Baptists of Virginia 1699-1926* (Richmond, Virginia: The Virginia Baptist Board of Missions and Education, 1955), p. 183.
14. *The First Annual Report of the Baptist Board of Foreign Missions, 1815,* p. 50.
15. *Proceedings of the Baptist Convention for Missionary Purposes,* 1814, p. 42.
16. *Proceedings of the General Convention of the Baptist Denomination in the United States,* 1817, p. 128.
17. Ibid.
18. *Proceedings of the Baptist Convention for Missionary Purposes,* 1814, p. 23.
19. Ibid., p. 39.
20. Ibid., p. 42.
21. Ibid.

4
Separation and Cooperation in Baptist Life

Baptist life contains elements which produce separation and encourage cooperation. Such tendencies are not of recent origin in a Baptist context. They have existed as dynamic sources of strength and weakness within the fellowship from the beginning. Many contemporary Baptists retain these concepts as valid principles but insist, nevertheless, upon evaluating and interpreting anew the implications involved in light of pressing demands created by modern society and probing questions raised by the Christian community.

A Heritage of Separation

A casual observer discovers quickly the Baptist propensity for separation. About thirty distinct Baptist groups maintain denominational structures in the United States. Terms, such as "Six-principle," "Primitive," "Conservative," "Southern," and "GARB," identify specific subgroups. Individuals, congregations, and general bodies normally reserve, at least unconsciously, the privilege of separation from every ecclesiastical relationship. Their Baptist heritage has convinced them that the possibility of separation is often closely allied with the desire for reformation.

John Smyth, the formative personality of early Baptist life, declared in 1609 that "ther is no way to reforme but to Seperate, as we have done already."[1] A former Anglican clergyman with Puritan sympathies, Smyth became a Separatist about 1606. Soon "differences" developed in the churches of the separation, which widened beyond repair when Smyth adopted believers' baptism (1609). Baptist churches appeared in England shortly afterward. Smyth's previous followers, Thomas Helwys and John Murton, continued the process of separation after Smyth sought union with the Mennonites. Later designated as General Baptists, they defended a general atonement and questioned various aspects of predestination.

Perhaps an undue emphasis has been placed upon the fact that Particular Baptists, who stressed a limited atonement and accepted the Calvinistic theological framework, arose from a "non-Separatist" tradition.[2] True, Henry Jacob established an "independent" congregation at Southwark, London, in 1616, from which several Congregational and Baptist churches originated. Individuals associated with this group rarely regarded the Church of England as totally false, and separations from the Jacob Church were usually congenial ones. Separations did occur, however, which often involved matters of deep conviction. When seven Baptist congregations that emerged from this context issued a doctrinal statement in 1644, it followed the pattern of an earlier Separatist confession. The articles involving baptism required believers' baptism by immersion and other significant articles defended congregational church polity, religious freedom, and lay-preaching.[3]

Both General and Particular Baptists immigrated to America, where often they united initially in one local fellowship. Controversy usually resulted which divided the congregation and perpetuated traditional theological differences. Baptist churches established at Providence (1639) and Newport (1644), Rhode Island, for example, experienced such divisions shortly after 1650. General Baptist churches declined in influence during the eighteenth century, however, and most of those remaining adopted Calvinistic confessions. The Philadelphia Association (established 1707) and the First Great Awakening played major roles in the transformation.

Baptist life originated, therefore, in separations which represented protests against state church establishments and prospects for regenerate churches. The Separate Baptist movement arose for similar reasons in New England, again reinforcing tendencies favoring separation in Baptist life. Expressing concern for pure churches and greater freedom, individuals and congregations, influenced by the First Great Awakening, formed about a hundred Strict Congregational churches. A large percentage of the latter group adopted Baptist principles, producing the Separate Baptist movement.[4] Isaac Backus progressed through the various stages indicated before leading New England Baptists in the struggle for religious freedom. Shubal Stearns and Daniel Marshall, also New England converts, settled at Sandy Creek, North Carolina, in 1755. From this strategic location, they spread the Separate Baptist witness throughout the South.[5] Assimilated gradually into the older Baptist fellowship, the Separates contributed an evangelistic outlook and a passion for freedom which generated much denominational activity in the following decades.

Motivated by evangelistic and missionary impulses, Baptists expanded westward in the United States and established congregations in other areas of the world during the nineteenth century. Significant separations continued, but their character changed markedly. Ecclesiastical, cultural, and theological issues fragmented the Baptist witness, encouraging individualism and sectarianism among the constituency. In the atmosphere of freedom, Baptists identified themselves as missionary or antimissionary, Northern or Southern, black or white, freewill or hardshell. Similar issues fragmented other American bodies also, indicating that nothing distinctively Baptistic created or prevented the disruptions. Rather than providing an appealing option, Baptists participated in what Franklin Littell designated "the scandal of indiscipline."[6] A strength grounded in principles designed to separate the churches from culture had now become a weakness dividing adherents of the principles over issues produced by the culture.

The first major division following the formation of national organizations was produced by the antimissions movement. Spokesmen John Taylor (1752-1835) of Kentucky, Daniel Parker (1781-1844) of Illinois and Indiana, and Alexander Campbell (1788-1866) of western Pennsylvania protested a growing centralization of Baptist life and attacked the activities of mission, Bible, and tract societies, Sunday Schools, theological seminaries, and so forth, as unscriptural. Followers of Campbell formed the nucleus for a developing Disciples movement. Primitive or Hard-shell Baptists emerged as strict Calvinist churches and associations which conferred, adopted resolutions, and distinguished themselves from fellow Baptists over a variety of issues. Diversity continues to characterize Primitive Baptists today, who number perhaps 120,000 members in about 3000 churches and a variety of loosely aligned denominational structures.[7]

More serious was the separation North and South that climaxed in 1845. The issue of slavery, with all its ramifications, fragmented the major American denominations before dividing the nation. A growing desire for abolition of slavery in the North and a vocal defense of the system in the South heightened tension around 1840 among Baptists in the national organizations. Control by moderate leaders prevailed until 1845, at which time neutrality proved impossible. Southerners organized the Southern Baptist Convention at Augusta, Georgia, in May 1845, locating their Foreign Mission Board at Richmond, Virginia, and their Domestic (Home) Mission Board at Marion, Alabama. Baptists of the North perpetuated the American Baptist Home Mission Society and restructured the foreign mission enterprise as the American Baptist Missionary Union. The Northern Baptist Convention was not formed until 1907, becoming the American Baptist Convention in 1950 and more recently (1979) the American Baptist Churches in the USA. Both Southern and American churches are found in all geographical areas of the United States, and dually aligned churches are not uncommon. Possibilities of reunion were discussed for several decades following the original separation, but no serious efforts have been made in this direction for a hundred years.[8]

Black Baptists for the most part worshiped in churches controlled by whites before the Civil War. Black congregations multiplied rapidly after the war, followed by associations, state conventions, and missionary organizations. Steps were taken toward a national structure when W. W. Colley led in forming the Baptist Foreign Mission Convention of the United States of America at Montgomery, Alabama, in 1880. Conventions to promote education and home missions appeared shortly afterward. These bodies merged in 1895 with the formation of The National Baptist Convention of the United States of America. Disputes over ownership and control of publishing activities divided this body in 1915 into the National Baptist Convention, USA, Inc. and the National Baptist Convention of America. The former fragmented further in 1961 amid controversy regarding tenure in office, a unified budget, and an executive secretary. The Progressive National Baptist Convention, Inc. resulted, establishing headquarters in Washington, D.C. Black Baptists affiliated with these three groups number almost ten million, constituting a sizable portion of the Baptist constituency in the United States.[9]

The Landmark movement led by J. R. Graves (1820-1893) not only heightened isolationist, exclusionist tendencies in the Southern Baptist Convention but also brought about some separations from the Convention. Graves remained within the Convention; but after his death, followers in the Southwest, particularly in Texas and Arkansas, formed (1905) what became (1924) the American Baptist Association with headquarters in Texarkana. Stressing that only local Baptist churches, existing in unbroken succession from the first century, possess authority from Christ to preach the gospel and administer his ordinances, the movement has been characterized as a Baptist high-church movement. Interpretation of the primacy of the local church fragmented this body in 1950 when some members refused to allow proxy representation at the association and withdrew to form the North American Baptist Association with headquarters at Little Rock, Arkansas. The latter body adopted the name Baptist Missionary Association of America in 1969. These two major Landmark groups number about a million and a half members at the present time.[10]

Fundamentalism further fragmented Baptists in the twentieth century, producing several small denominations. Major groups that withdrew from the Northern Baptist Convention included the General Association of Regular Baptists formed at Chicago, Illinois, in 1932 and the Conservative Baptist Association of America organized at Atlantic City, New Jersey, in 1947. J. Frank Norris (1881-1952) attacked activities of the Southern Baptist Convention for three decades, and the World Baptist Fellowship (and later the Bible Baptist Fellowship) resulted from these efforts. In addition, hundreds of "independent" churches pursued goals and developed programs without formal attachment to any structure beyond the local church.[11]

Smaller Baptist bodies have retained a separate identity even when issues that produced them declined in importance. *Seventh-Day* and *Freewill, Two-Seed-in-the-Spirit Predestinarian* and *United, Separate* and *Regular, Six-principle* and *Duck River* are terms familiar to the stu-

dent of Baptist history. Also, linguistic and cultural differences have insured that Baptist groups, such as those of German (North American
Baptist General Conference) or Swedish (Baptist General Conference)
background, have retained distinctive organizations, increasing the
number of denominational entities in the Baptist fellowship.[12] A propensity for separation is ingrained in the Baptist heritage.

A Record of Cooperation

A series of separations influenced the origin, character, and development of Baptist life. At the same time, however, those involved evidenced a high regard for cooperation, avoiding individual anarchy or
group isolation whenever possible. "Baptists from the beginning,"
observed the British historian W. T. Whitley, "sought to maintain sisterly
intercourse between local churches; they never thought that one church
was independent of others."[13] Associations linked the earliest churches
together very quickly, and before long general assemblies and other
organizations extended ecclesiastical boundaries. "Associations,
Synods, Unions and Assemblies of churches are not to be regarded as
optional and secondary," commented Ernest Payne. "They are the
necessary expression of Christian fellowship, a necessary manifestation
of the Church visible."[14] Early Baptists cooperated, and the principle of
working together has remained in denominational life as it has extended
into other countries and different centuries until the present.

As might be expected, Baptists cooperated more readily among themselves than with others. In spite of internal differences, their achieve-
ments in cooperation with each other have been rather remarkable. The
Baptist World Alliance, formed in 1905, provides an international organization designed to show "the essential oneness of Baptist people in
the Lord Jesus Christ, to impart inspiration to the brotherhood, and to
promote the spirit of fellowship, service, and cooperation among its
members."[15] In fulfilling this stated purpose, the Alliance supports a
program involving communications, relief, religious liberty, study and
research, and international meetings. Its membership (1979) includes
111 national conventions/unions with 29 million members scattered
throughout 120 countries.[16] "They do not know us who say we are
mere individualists," declared J. H. Rushbrooke, the first general secre-

tary. "Individualists we are, standing for the supreme value and the solemn and separate responsibility of every human soul; isolated we are not, for in him we are indissolubly united. The Baptist World Alliance," he continued, "demonstrates that our policy has room for the unforced expression of an inward and spiritual unity which no human scheme can either create or destroy."[17] More than 20,000 participants from the world family of Baptists attended the Fourteenth Congress which convened July 8-13, 1980, in Toronto, Canada.

Seven Baptist conventions in North America jointly celebrated the 150th anniversary of organized Baptist life on a national scale in Atlantic City in May, 1964. The celebration was preceded by a six-year regional program known as the Baptist Jubilee Advance. Encouraged by these endeavors, the joint committee representing the conventions proposed the formation of a North American Fellowship. "The North American Baptist Fellowship is based upon the thinking that Baptists in North America have a great deal in common and can work together for a common good," commented a later chairperson. "We have beliefs and interests in common, and we also have some problems in common. Such differences as occur, which are often those of emphasis, can serve as challenges rather than grounds for division."[18] The European Baptist Federation functions in a similar capacity for that area, as do similar agencies in the Caribbean, Asia, and Latin America. These continental fellowships operate under the umbrella of the Alliance in encouraging interaction and cooperation among Baptists in their respective areas.

The Baptists' desire for fellowship has been equaled or surpassed by their concern for freedom. "No denomination has its roots more firmly planted in the soil of religious freedom and Church-State separation than the Baptists,"[19] commented Anson Phelps Stokes, who attributed Baptists' unusual influence "mainly to religious conviction."[20] In behalf of religious freedom, therefore, Baptists have cooperated not only with other Christians but also with those professing other religions or no religion.

The Baptist Joint Committee on Public Affairs located in Washington, D.C., and supported by nine conventions serves as an effective instrument for communication, interpretation, and negotiation on matters involving religious liberty. Few major Baptist meetings adjourn without adopting some statement related directly or indirectly to the issue. "The Baptist interest in church-state separation," asserted Thomas G. Sanders, "has led them to enter P.O.A.U. (now Americans United) in large numbers and furnish it with much of its leadership."[21] Baptist support for Americans United has not diminished in recent years. Almost any group or agency involved in promoting or protecting religious freedom receives strong support from Baptists, who regard themselves as among the major religious defenders of this tradition in America.

Baptist life has been characterized also by a commitment to Christian unity. Interpretations regarding specific implications of this conviction, however, have varied considerably, as have cooperative responses based upon these implications. Several Baptist groups in the United States participate actively in the National Council of Churches. Others cooperate with alternative organizations such as the National Association of Evangelicals or the American Council of Christian Churches. Still others avoid these or similar ecumenical alliances, denying that Christian unity requires such organized expression. Baptists respond essentially in the same patterns toward international and world organizations, reflecting diverse interpretations and different degrees of involvement.

The Southern Baptist Convention illustrates the latter category described, for a remarkably consistent philosophy has undergirded most Convention pronouncements on ecumenical relations. Expressed clearly in the 1925 statement of faith and reaffirmed in 1963, the article on cooperation declared:

Christian unity in the New Testament sense is spiritual harmony and voluntary co-operation for common ends by various groups of Christ's people. Co-operation is desirable between the various Christian denominations when the end to be attained is itself justified, and when such co-operation involves no violation of conscience or compromise of loyalty to Christ and his Word as revealed in the New Testament.[22]

Unity should be interpreted in terms of "spiritual harmony" and "voluntary co-operation." Specific cooperative endeavors should be encouraged which involve neither a violation of conscience nor a compromise of principles. Although the ecumenical movement has influenced the Convention by its emphasis upon Christian unity, Southern Baptists remain unconvinced that unity implies interdenominational structures or organic unions in any way.[23] They are fully persuaded that a functional approach to denominationalism and a spiritual harmony approach to Christian unity fulfill New Testament requirements adequately.

The Convention faces an era that will probably demand further examination and clarification of these approaches. Southern Baptists have insisted that their Convention has "no ecclesiological authority. It is in no sense the Southern Baptist Church."[24] Paul Minear, a Yale University professor, noted "sound theological reasons" why earlier Christians rejected such a designation for their denominations.

There is, for instance, no scriptural ground or warrant for calling our denominations churches. Moreover, it becomes increasingly difficult for the historian to link a particular denomination to the biblical images of the people of God (e.g. the body of Christ), to the key phrases in the creeds and confessions (e.g. the communion of saints), and to the *notae ecclesiae*.[25]

Most Southern Baptists would agree with these and other reasons cited.

In spite of areas of agreement, Minear and others are not adopting a Southern Baptist point of view. As functional, administrative entities, denominations cannot command the highest loyalties. "The denominational form of organization cannot thrive long after devoted men dissociate loyalty to Christ from loyalty to that form."[26] His conclusion follows naturally. "Perhaps in an age that will be truly ecumenical it will be the destiny of all denominations to decrease so that the church may increase."[27] Denominations, he feels, are functional and therefore unnecessary and should be abandoned in favor of the church.

Within the Convention similar problems are appearing. A cohesive community with a strong sense of purpose encounters relatively few difficulties involving unity. As the community expands, however, or the sense of purpose weakens, fragmentation often occurs. In this context "functional" easily becomes "optional," especially when accompanied by a widespread individualism. The Convention, which extends presently into all fifty states and encompasses a vast diversity of backgrounds and viewpoints, is already experiencing situations of this type. The strongest loyalties of the constituency are attached to the local congregations and to the church. This will likely remain unchanged, as will the functional interpretation of the denomination. Implications of the latter will need to be explored further, however, especially in terms of relations between the congregations and the denomination and between the denomination and the church.

The "spiritual harmony" approach to Christian unity may likewise require additional clarification in the near future. For many individuals, the concept is so vague that it encourages a passive or even a negative attitude. In one sense, Wayne Dehoney is correct in asserting that "a denomination *is* an ecumenical structure!"[28] But when several hundred such structures actively compete for loyalty and support on the American scene, "harmony" becomes rather elusive.

Present trends reflect little evidence that Southern Baptists will participate in existing ecumenical organizations, such as the World or National Councils of Churches or in merger negotiations such as the Consultation on Church Union. In different ways, however, and at many levels the Convention has become a truly national organization with the largest non-Catholic membership in America. Consequently, it will become increasingly difficult to maintain an isolationist stance. Creative activities will likely be promoted as clear demands of spiritual harmony.

Many Southern Baptists agree with Wayne Dehoney that "we should not and cannot ignore the challenge of the surging ecumenical spirit in Christendom."[29] Precisely how the Convention should face this challenge, however, presents some difficulties. It appears that individuals and groups concerned with the matter should address attention to three specific demands at this time.

First, they should develop and perpetuate an awareness of the tremendous indebtedness of Southern Baptists to the total Christian movement in history. The Southern Baptist Convention has functioned effectively for 135 years, but the statement could accurately read for *only* 135 years. The Convention heritage contains contributions not only from previous Baptist groups but also from the totality of the Christian movement. When Southern Baptists invoke "the blessings of the triune God upon all who name the name of our Lord Jesus Christ,"[30] they must be reminded of a large segment of Christian truth shared with others. Individuals at times affirm the sole authority of Scripture, defend "Calvinistic" theology or a "Zwinglian" interpretation of the Lord's

Supper, and uphold "congregational" church government while denying or modifying a Protestant heritage for Baptists. From German Piet-
ism, the Wesleyan revivals, and a series of awakenings in America,
Southern Baptists inherited passions for evangelism and missions which
have been driving forces in denominational life. "We are debtors,"
declared Paul, and the affirmation reflected his greatness rather than
detracting from it. Southern Baptists are indebted to the total Christian
tradition.

Second, Southern Baptists should give renewed attention to the matter of distinctiveness or uniqueness in their life and thought. At stake will
be the very reason for existence as a separate denomination. Statements stressing a distinctive witness often impress the thoughtful observer by their lack of distinctiveness. Most Christian groups, for example, affirm and believe that their essential doctrines are based upon the
Bible. In areas where Baptists have made outstanding contributions in
the past, such as religious freedom and a regenerate church regulated
by believers' baptism and discipline, Southern Baptists reflect considerable uncertainty and unconcern. Several contemporary spokesmen
have advanced a promising concept, namely that the denomination
could fulfill a unique role in interpreting and demonstrating the proper
balance between evangelism and social concern. Further, an increasingly impersonal world might listen attentively to an articulate expression of a faith that is personal in nature and approach but not radically
individualistic. Diverse areas might be noted by different interpreters, but
most Southern Baptists evidently believe that their denomination has
something to offer at this time. The present age demands precise definition and consistent demonstration of the content involved in that "something."

A third demand is closely related to the second. How may Southern
Baptists best share what they have to offer with other Christians and the
world? Equally important, how may other Christians and the world best
share what they have to offer with Southern Baptists? These are not
easy questions, and diverse approaches have been suggested. As
already noted, some leaders have advocated a limited participation in
existing ecumenical organizations, and others have advised the creation
of additional structures. A unilateral approach would probably be pre-

ferred by most but that which is offered in this way is often rejected, and little is received in reverse.

An urbanized, secularized, overpopulated, technological world may call the Christian community back to central concerns, to truly vital issues. A German Baptist leader noted that "on the European continent the ecumenical question no longer belongs to those questions which create excitement among young people—and not only among them." His analysis called attention to "a pre-ecumenical church confronted with a post-Christian world."[31] As in the past, Southern Baptist concern for the world should motivate the devising of new ways of sharing and receiving that which is vital to the Christian witness.

Conclusion

An influential manual of polity and practice asserts that the "most distinctive emphasis" of Baptists has been a threefold solution of what Emil Brunner called "the unsolved problem of the Reformation."[32] How is the one *church* related to the many separate churches? First, Baptists believed that the churches should reproduce as nearly as possible the life which characterizes the *church*. Second, they accepted the primacy of the *church* but insisted that individual churches represent the larger body in a particular locality and possess all essential powers of self-government. Third, they devised ways to express the interdependence of the local churches in order to avoid any tendency toward isolated self-sufficiency.[33]

Ideally, the above solution regards separation and cooperation as complementary concepts. By insisting that individual churches reproduce the life and retain the powers of the church, Baptists defend the principle of separation. In acknowledging interdependence and avoiding isolated self-sufficiency, they encourage cooperation. In actual practice, of course, the two conflict often, especially when separation occurs within the churches or when cooperation disregards cherished convictions. But the distinctive quality of life envisioned in the principle of separation should enhance rather than preclude cooperation in Christ.

Notes

1. John Smyth, *Parallels, Censures, Observations* in *The Works of John Smyth*, W. T. Whitley, II, ed. (Cambridge: University Press, 1915), p. 345.
2. See Winthrop S. Hudson, ed., *Baptist Concepts of the Church* (Chicago: The Judson Press, 1959), p. 13. See also B. R. White, *The English Separatist Tradition* (Oxford: University Press, 1971) and Murray Tolmie, *The Triumph of the Saints* (Cambridge: Cambridge University Press, 1977).
3. Cf. William L. Lumpkin, *Baptist Confessions of Faith* (Chicago: The Judson Press, 1959), pp. 153-171.
4. Cf. C. C. Goen, *Revivalism and Separatism in New England, 1740-1800* (New Haven: Yale University Press, 1962), pp. 208 *ff.*
5. Cf. William L. Lumpkin, *Baptist Foundations in the South* (Nashville: Broadman Press, 1961), pp. 33 *ff.*
6. Franklin H. Littell, *From State Church to Pluralism* (Garden City, New York: Doubleday and Company, Inc., 1962), p. 119.
7. Cf. Arthur Carl Piepkorn, "The Primitive Baptists of North America," *Baptist History and Heritage,* 7 (January, 1972), pp. 33-51.
8. See Robert Andrew Baker, *Relations Between Northern and Southern Baptists* (Fort Worth: 2nd edition, Marvin D. Evans Printing Company, 1954); Robert A. Baker, *The Southern Baptist Convention and Its People 1607-1972* (Nashville: Broadman Press, 1974); Samuel S. Hill, Jr. and Robert G. Torbet, *Baptists North and South* (Valley Forge: The Judson Press, 1963); and Robert Handy, "American Baptist Polity: What's Happening and Why," *Baptist History and Heritage,* 14 (July, 1979), pp. 12-21.
9. Cf. Davis Collier Woolley, ed., *Baptist Advance* (Nashville: Broadman Press, 1964).
10. See *Baptist History and Heritage,* X (January, 1975) for excellent discussions of varied aspects of the Landmark movement.
11. Cf. E. Ray Tatum, *Conquest or Failure? Biography of J. Frank Norris* (Dallas, Texas: Baptist Historical Foundation, 1966) and Walter B. Shurden, *Not a Silent People* (Nashville: Broadman Press, 1972).
12. See Davis Collier Woolley, ed., *Baptist Advance* (Nashville: Broadman Press, 1964).
13. W. T. Whitley, *A History of British Baptists* (London: Chas. Griffin and Co., 1923), p. 86 *ff.*
14. Ernest A. Payne, *The Fellowship of Believers* (London: The Carey Kingsgate Press, Ltd., 1954), p. 31.
15. *Annual,* Southern Baptist Convention, 1979, p. 207.
16. Ibid.
17. Cited by Josef Nordenhaug, "The Essential Unity of the Baptist People," *Review and Expositor,* LXII (Spring, 1965), p. 158.

18. Cited by James D. Mosteller, "Inter-Baptist Ecumenism," *Review and Expositor,* LXVI (Summer, 1969), p. 284.
19. Anson Phelps Stokes, *Church and State in the United States,* III (New York: Harper and Brother , 1950), p. 485.
20. Ibid.
21. Thomas G. Sanders, *Protestant Concepts of Church and State* (Garden City, New York: Doubleday and Company, Inc., 1965), p. 230.
22. Robert A. Baker, ed., *A Baptist Source Book* (Nashville: Broadman Press, 1966), p. 210.
23. Cf. William R. Estep, *Baptists and Christian Unity* (Nashville: Broadman Press, 1966) and Claude L. Howe, Jr., "Southern Baptists and the Ecumenical Movement," *The Theological Educator,* 1 (October, 1970), pp. 30-36.
24. Baker, p. 211.
25. Paul Minear, "The Church, Ecumenism, and Methodism," in *Methodism's Destiny in an Ecumenical Age,* Paul M. Minus, Jr., ed. (Nashville: Abingdon Press, 1969), p. 41.
26. Ibid., p. 38.
27. Ibid., p. 43.
28. Wayne Dehoney, "Southern Baptists and Ecumenism: Options for the Future," *Review and Expositor,* LXVI (Summer, 1969), p. 317.
29. Ibid., 313.
30. Baker, p. 211.
31. Otmar Schulz, "Baptists and the Ecumenical Movement," *Review and Expositor,* LXVI (Summer, 1969), p. 264.
32. Norman H. Maring and Winthrop S. Hudson, *A Baptist Manual of Polity and Practice* (Valley Forge, Pa.: The Judson Press, 1963), p. 36.
33. Ibid.

5

William Newton Clarke: Baptist Theologian of Theological Liberalism

The last decade of the nineteenth century was a crucial period for American Christianity in general and for American theology in particular. The New England theology, which united Calvinism and revivalism into "a rationally coherent and defensible system,"[1] had been the leading Protestant tradition in this country. However, its inability to cope with the scientific and historical movements, principally evolutionary thought and biblical criticism, and its indifference to the emerging social demands of an industrial society made its collapse "sudden and devastating."[2] Traditional Calvinism continued to survive, but "it was consciously on the defensive."[3]

Theological liberalism emerged gradually out of a vacuum created by the collapse of the New England theology. By 1890 liberal theologians accepted evolution with its implications, as well as the principle of biblical criticism and some of its results, while modifying many traditional concepts, such as endless future punishment and the understanding of the person and work of Christ. However, Frank Hugh Foster has noted,

no comprehensive and truly great theologian had appeared to write a theology which should steady Christian thinking, conserve the results already gained, systematize the statements of truth and show its inner harmony, and open a clear path upon which theologians might advance with a reasonable hope of attaining a still wider and more exact view of the eternal truth.[4]

When William Newton Clarke published *An Outline of Christian Theology* in 1898, he did not have these particular objectives in mind; but his book "was immediately received with the greatest satisfaction by the advancing liberalism, and attained a circulation and an influence which marked it as one of the great books of the time."[5]

The immediate reception and appropriation of the basic tenets of Clarke's theological system by liberal theologians can easily be understood. Clarke accepted without question both biblical criticism and theistic evolution, while the place of primacy he gave to Christian experience accorded with the liberal outlook. In fact, his theological system was basically a traditional orthodoxy, modified by new views of the Bible and the universe, and reinterpreted in the light of Christian experience.

Clarke's intensely personal theology must be undersood as an expression of religious convictions that arose out of years of meditation and study as a Christian student, minister, and teacher. Reared and trained in a Baptist atmosphere, he preached and taught in Baptist institutions most of his life. Sharing the conservative theological outlook of a majority of his denominational contemporaries for many years, he responded slowly to forces that brought about a theological transition in this country. At last he became the first systematic theologian of theological liberalism in America. A strange mixture of conservatism and liberalism in his thought is accounted for by this gradual development.

Early Life

The second son of Baptist minister William Clarke and Urania Miner, William Newton Clarke was born December 2, 1841, at Cazenovia, New York. In this devout Christian home, the young man developed a deep appreciation for the Bible and accepted a "mitigated form of Calvinism"[6] as the proper interpretation of Christian truth. Receiving his secondary education at the Oneida Conference Seminary in Cazenovia, Clarke imbibed the "warm and demonstrative qualities of Methodism."[7] His personal religious experience began during one of the frequent revivals that swept the campus. Developing a scholastic interest in languages, the conscientious student studied Latin, Greek, and German under a capable teacher. He graduated in the spring of 1858 as the youngest member in a class of twelve students and was admitted the following fall as a sophomore to Madison University (later Colgate University) in Hamilton, New York.

Responding to a liberal education while at Madison, Clarke added Spanish to a growing list of languages at his command. The young collegian also matured religiously, surrendering to the ministerial call during his last semester, and participated frequently in "recreation, reading, and good fellowship."[8] Many of his classmates enlisted in the Union Army after graduation in 1861, but Clarke's physical condition would not allow him to participate in the conflict. Therefore, he enrolled in Hamilton Theological Seminary to prepare for his life commitment.

Two teachers at the seminary, Hezekiah Harvey and Ebenezer Dodge, influenced Clarke decisively. For Harvey "the voice of the Bible was the voice of God, and therefore he bent his ear to listen."[9] A careful exegete and an avid exponent of textual criticism, Harvey felt that his Christian duty was to restore and understand the words of the biblical autographs. Completely captivated by this teacher, whose "influence and example" made him "a Bible student,"[10] Clarke described Harvey as "a good scholar" and a "man of strong convictions, of a most beautiful devoutness, of absolute sincerity, and of perfectly unconquerable industry."[11] In contrast, Dodge "ranged more widely, he was more mystical in his vein, and he was more of a philosopher, thinking for himself and outreaching far and wide."[12] Revolting against this different approach of Dodge, who had recently spent fifteen months in Europe studying under Tholuck and Dorner, young Clarke adopted the outlook of Harvey. A quirk of history, however, is that within three decades, he succeeded Dodge, his theology professor, and wrote concerning his approach to theology: "My life had brought me entirely over to the position of my early teacher in theology, now my predecessor, from whose method I had so conscientiously dissented in my youth."[13]

Preacher and Exegete

After graduating from the seminary in 1863, Clarke accepted his first pastorate at Keene, New Hampshire. His father preached an appropriate ordination sermon in January 1864. For the next quarter century the younger Clarke devoted his life primarily to pastoral duties.

Keene, the county seat and a New England town of about four thousand residents, offered excellent opportunities both for service and training. No radical changes took place in Clarke's thought during this six-year pastorate. But ideas and insights unconsciously planted developed later into theological concepts greatly different from those which he advocated at this time.

The studious pastor continued meticulously studying the Bible and sought to involve his congregation in systematic training. Besides preaching a series of "Bible Sermons"[14] for an extended period of time, Clarke worked consistently to master the Greek New Testament, which was compared with Latin, German, and French translations.[15] As might be expected, Clarke's interests were exegetical rather than theological. He felt that most theological problems could be solved by proper biblical exegesis.

The church at Keene, like many other churches in New England, "had suffered sadly from the Millerite excitement, expecting the second coming of Christ in 1843, and all the intervening years had not been sufficient to wear out the ill effects."[16] Experience with this movement taught Clarke the danger of strictly literalistic biblical interpretation and made him much more susceptible in later years to a radically different type of eschatological thought.

During this period, the Baptist pastor first seriously encountered evolutionary thought. Requested by the local ministerial club to give a critique of the concept as advocated by Herbert Spencer, Clarke repudiated Spencer's argument, using principally the proof-text method. Although "impressed by the simplicity and massiveness of the idea, and by the almost boundless wealth of illustration that Spencer was able to bring to its service,"[17] Clarke felt that "the doctrine was in contradiction to the Scriptures, and that stood as reason enough for leaving it aside."[18] Clarke rejected evolution because it appeared to contradict the Bible; but when his views regarding the Bible changed, he immediately adopted evolutionary thought as an integral part of his theology.

Clarke accepted the pastorate of the First Baptist Church at Newton Centre, Massachusetts, in May 1869, and married Emily A. Smith that September. The young couple faced many tasks together, but this first mutual endeavor appeared the most exacting since Newton Centre was the home of Newton Theological Institution, whose faculty and students comprised a significant part of the Baptist congregation.

The type of scholarly work required at Newton Centre kept Clarke close to his Bible and to his pen. For the next eleven years, every text was carefully exegeted with the help of the best available commentaries. Every sermon was written out completely and read from a manuscript.

This latter exercise aided in developing a beautiful, clear, and somewhat homiletical style for which Clarke later became famous, while the first brought him into contact with the best biblical scholarship of his day.

Alvah Hovey, president and professor of theology at Newton Theological Institution, exerted the greatest personal influence upon Clarke during this period. Hovey had been chairman of the pulpit committee that selected the new pastor, who "immediately won and held a very high place in the esteem and love of the older man."[19] Theologically, the following description that Clarke gave of Hovey after his death in 1903 could as easily have been made in 1870.

He held that the substance of theology consists of the systematized contents of the Bible. In the Bible, he thought, God had made a sufficient revelation of himself, and of the truth in religion with which men are concerned. The work of the theologian is the drawing out, arranging, expounding, and illustrating of this divinely-given material.[20]

E. P. Gould, the progressively liberal professor of New Testament interpretation, balanced this conservative influence, while other liberalizing factors worked more or less unconsciously to lure Clarke away from his inherited tradition. Discussions current in that day on the premillennial and postmillennial theories of the second advent of Christ convinced him that both theories could be equally supported by the Bible. This conviction naturally involved his attitude toward both the Bible and the advent. He later wrote:

At first I did not see how much this meant, but gradually it came to me, and a very important change in my convictions was a necessary result. It was borne in upon me that the Bible contains material for two opposite and irreconcilable doctrines about the early return of Chist to this world.[21]

By far Clarke's most important development at Newton Centre, however, concerned the doctrine of the person and work of Christ. For a short time, Clarke came under the influence of various books on the life of Christ. One by Frederick W. Farrar, "despite its faults," particularly gave him "a powerful impulse toward conceiving Jesus Christ as real."[22] But in the area of the atonement the most marked change occurred.

Soon after Clarke's arrival at Newton Centre, he carefully studied *The Vicarious Sacrifice Grounded in Principles of Universal Obligation* by Horace Bushnell. A highly critical review of this book by Alvah Hovey stirred his initial interest. "The genius and personality of the author (Bushnell) impressed him more than his teaching, yet Clarke could never afterward see the doctrine of the atonement in precisely the same light as before."[23] Several years later Clarke began "that independent study of the doctrine of the atonement which was to lead him away from the traditional static view of theology and make him a recognized interpreter of a new day."[24] Although growing naturally out of an exegetical problem, the investigation could not be confined to the realm of exegesis. When it ended, Clarke's basic theological conceptions were firmly fixed. Concerning this experience, he later wrote:

For months I was held to my task by a power from which there was no escape —from which indeed I had no desire to escape. It was a great experience; for now, under an impulse that I knew to be from God, my best powers were for the first time grappling with the prime moral facts of existence. I had been handling divine realities all my years, but never until now had I been under such strong and joyful constraint in dealing with them. Such labor could not be in vain in the Lord, and to me it was richly fruitful.[25]

Clarke sought to clarify this crucial Christian doctrine in his own mind by reading what others had written and by carefully studying the Bible. When this approach did not yield satisfactory results, he resorted to the experiential method that later became so predominant in his theology. The basic convictions under which he worked were that God consistently and eternally acted in accord with his own character and that this character was revealed in Jesus Christ. Clarke attempted to isolate, therefore, "the ethical principles of the divine character, which the Christian revelation has brought to light."[26] Nothing was allowed to remain in the doctrine that did not conform to these principles. The Bible served as his "indispensable and invaluable helper in the quest,"[27] but he used it not so much "in the light of its statements"[28] as "in the light of its principles."[29]

The change in Clarke's theological outlook that resulted from this study could not help influencing his preaching. Many of his parishioners resented an increasingly ethical note that gradually replaced the biblicist approach to which they were accustomed. Therefore, he welcomed a call to the Olivet Baptist Church of Montreal, Canada, moving to this new field of endeavor in 1880.

Clarke's change of position agreed with the change in the man, for Montreal "was the most cosmopolitan environment of any place of his residence and his mind expanded with the broader outlook upon life."[30] Immediately relinquishing the practice of reading his sermons, he exercised an equal liberty in other directions.

The ethical concept of the character of God as revealed in Christ gradually permeated the whole of Clarke's theology. It become as dominant as the concept of the sovereignty of God had been in the theology of John Calvin. At the same time, Clarke came more and more to rely upon Christian experience as the verifier of truth. Writing to a friend in 1881, he contended that

the real truth is of a high and comprehensive kind and is to be reached not so much by close analysis and exclusion as by a process indescribable, with which the heart has quite as much to do as the intellect . . . . It is an experience of God, and the more fully the whole being of man is involved in that experience . . . the more truly and justly shall we know the truth of God.[31]

A little later he wrote: "I have come to feel more and more that 'what is true is safe,' and that what I can spiritually trust as true will not lead me astray."[32]

Clarke realized that his theological journey was taking him gradually away from the traditional Baptist viewpoint. In April 1881, he wrote: "I do not regard myself as a champion of denominational orthodoxy, but I do regard myself as a Baptist and as a humble champion of my Master's truth."[33] This seems to have remained his attitude toward the denomination. Although repeatedly exercising that element of personal freedom for which Baptists had historically stood, Clarke urged many young men, during this period and until his death, to remain within the denomination even if some of their convictions differed basically from those of the majority of the group.

Shortly after moving to Montreal, Clarke received a request from his old friend, Alvah Hovey, to write a *Commentary on the Gospel of Mark* for the series, *An American Commentary on the New Testament,* of which Hovey was general editor. Published in 1881 after Hovey had deleted some incidental comments on the inspiration of the Scriptures, the book received its most severe criticisms over the doctrine of eschatology. Clarke interpreted the entire thirteenth chapter of Mark as referring to the fall of Jerusalem without reference to the second coming of Christ. In a second edition of the work, the editor inserted "an additional view," which set forth the traditional interpretation desired.[34]

Clarke fell and injured a knee in the winter of 1883. Even after many weeks in bed, he found his pastoral duties extremely difficult to perform. It seemed providential, therefore, when he was asked to teach New Testament interpretation at Toronto Baptist College. Before the final decision, however, Clarke frankly discussed his view of the Bible and of theology with President John H. Castle, who assured him that this in no way affected the offer. Encouraging those under his direction "to be correct and faithful in their handling of the Bible, and to put it to no use inconsistent with its original intention,"[35] the new professor freely expressed his own views and contributed to his students the fruit of many years of careful exegesis and devotional Bible study.

The injured knee continued to plague him. "After that not a single year passed without some mishap, slight or serious, due to the lame, uncertain knee."[36] In June 1884, he fell and permanently injured his right elbow, which necessitated his learning to write with his left hand. He accepted this double disability without undue complaint however. When the pastorate at the church at Hamilton, New York, was offered to him early in 1887, Clarke felt able to assume demanding pastoral duties at the scene of his college and seminary training.

Always preeminently a preacher, Clarke returned to this work with great joy. The faculty and students of the college and the seminary offered a challenge he eagerly accepted. Several of his teachers, including Dodge and Harvey, were numbered among his parishioners.

The results of textual criticism had been used by Clarke throughout his ministry. After returning to Hamilton, he responded favorably to many conclusions advocated by higher criticism and felt that they "largely unified and Christianized" his Bible.[37] In his thinking, these results removed most of the moral difficulties in the Old Testament and showed that the inward and spiritual message of the prophets was the heart of religion before, as well as after, the time of Christ.

Clarke's teacher and friend, Ebenezer Dodge, died suddenly during January 1890. Requested to devote a portion of his time to teaching theology for the remainder of the school year, Clarke unexpectedly found himself again in the classroom. He took his new duties very seriously, as is indicated by a letter to Alvah Hovey the following March.

I wish to be sincere, and I pray that I may do good and not evil to those whom I thus touch. If I have my wish with my young men, they will see more of God, and have a warmer heart toward Christ, and be more thoroughly their own best selves in all their thinking, for my presence among them.[38]

At the close of the school year, the temporary position became a permanent one. Clarke resigned his church to accept the J. J. Joslin Professorship of Christian Theology. Continuing to preach when opportunities presented themselves, he devoted the rest of his life primarily to the work of a teacher and theologian.

Teacher and Theologian

The task to which Clarke committed himself was not an easy one, for his theological outlook by this time vastly differed from that of many of his colleagues and most of his students. He used the printed theological text of his predecessor to complete the unfinished term of work. However, necessity, because the supply of these books was exhausted, and honesty, because the ideas contained therein were not his own, compelled him to begin at once to formulate a system of theology in agreement with the principles that he had adopted.

Besides his major course in theology, Clarke taught classes in missions, comparative religion, ethics, and apologetics. Most of his constructive effort in the first few years, however, was devoted to the writing of *An Outline of Christian Theology*. After four revisions, this work was privately printed in 1894 and published after a fifth revision in 1898. Although it "brought down upon him the invectives of the orthodox,"[39] its general reception was immediate and overwhelming. William H. Allison has written:

This was an epoch-making book, for it was the first broad survey of Christian theology which frankly accepted the modern view of the world, substituted vital, dynamic phraseology for the mechanical and static, and subordinated theology to the Christian religion itself, which was to be discerned both by a historical approach to the Scriptures and by the experiential evidence of all times.[40]

The favorable reception of Clarke's first book on theology opened the door for a series of lectures and similar books. This firmly established him as a significant leader among liberal thinkers of this country and Great Britain. Invited to lecture at the Harvard University School of Theology in 1899, he soon published his lectures under the title *Can I Believe in God the Father?* Later the same year his Levering Lectures to Johns Hopkins University appeared in the work *What Shall We Think of Christianity?* He delivered the Nathaniel William Taylor Lectures at Yale Divinity School in 1905, which were published as *The Use of the Scriptures in Theology.* Before his death, Clarke had spoken at Oberlin College, Andover Theological Seminary, and many other schools of higher learning in the United States.

Besides producing several popular books and accepting many invitations to lecture, Clarke also received recognition through the honorary degrees conferred upon him by Yale University in 1900 and the University of Chicago in 1901. These were suppplemented by the degree of Doctor of Sacred Theology, which Columbia University conferred upon him in 1910.

Clarke's health was not good for several years. In 1904, he arranged to teach his classes each year in the spring and fall terms, which allowed him to spend the winter months in Deland, Florida, where he worked almost daily at the library of Stetson University. After June 1908, even this arrangement proved too demanding. He resigned his professorship in theology, but the school provided a lectureship in Christian ethics so they could retain his services. This gave Clarke more free time, which he used mostly for writing.

Clarke began *The Christian Doctrine of God* for *The International Theological Library* series while on a pleasure trip to Europe in 1901. He abandoned that particular approach and began anew after returning to this country in 1902. This book demanded much of his free time for several years and was not published until 1909. *Sixty Years with the Bible* appeared later the same year, and *The Ideal of Jesus* was completed in 1911. Clarke's last lecture, "Immortality: A Study of Belief," was delivered at Yale Divinity School before departing for his winter home in Deland, where he experienced another fall which took his life on January 14, 1912.

Theological Perspective

William Newton Clarke developed convictions concerning the Bible, the universe, and Christian experience that not only led him away from the theological outlook of his youth but also provided major principles around which a new theology was formulated. Strict adherence to these principles gave his thought a remarkable unity and consistency. At many points, one is inclined to give mental assent to proposed conclusions simple because they correspond so precisely with the system in its totality.

Although not the only source of theology, the Scriptures must be used as its major source, but "they must be used for what they are."[41] To Clarke this meant that the results of critical inquiry should be freely received. Accepting a modified biblical authority which he refused to base upon any doctrine of infallible inspiration, Clarke contended that

the AUTHORITY of the Scriptures is the authority of the truth that they convey. The Scriptures are authoritative to us because they contain the highest moral and religious truth, which has the right to satisfy our reason and bind our conscience.[42]

Firmly believing that "Christian theology must be all Christian,"[43] Clarke applied this concept to the elements which theology should receive from the Bible. "The Christian element in the Scriptures is the indispensable and formative element in Christian theology," he contended, "and is the only element in the Scriptures which Christian theology is either required or permitted to receive as contributing to its substance."[44] By "the Christian element," Clarke meant that "which enters into or accords with the view of divine realities which Jesus Christ revealed."[45] Defining this element further as "a body of spiritual reality put into life,"[46] the liberal theologian had in mind not the words or teachings of Jesus as such, but the total contribution of Jesus to religious thought and experience concerning God and his relation to man.

How may one locate the Christian element in the Bible? To this question Clarke replied:

The way to identify the Christian element is taught by its nature . . . . Evidence is to be in the thing itself, not in its locality or its label. Inspiration was an outward mark, but the inward certifier is quality; and quality can certify itself only by appeal to judgment, or discernment. Quality must be recognized: there is no other way.[47]

This contention, that theology must be "all Christian," ensured that Clarke's system would be centered in Christ. Applying to every potential doctrine of theology the same test that he applied to biblical passages, he admitted what was felt to be specifically Christian. His point of departure was not the person or work of Christ, however, but the character of God as revealed by Christ. The belief that God was and always had been, within himself and toward all men, such a being as Christ revealed increasingly dominated his theology and gave to it an ethical consistency which was perhaps the most unique element in his thought.

Henry P. Van Dusen has identified the principle of continuity as "the major positive principle of the liberal mind."[48] Clarke exemplifies this statement, for he thought of God and men as alike, of science and revelation as similar, and of all religions as expressions of the religious nature of man. Stating that "the doctrine of evolution declares the unity and continuity of things,"[49] Clarke sought to create a theology that would comply with its demands. His evolutionary concept of the universe and its application to theology, however, demonstrated no real originality or uniqueness. It simply reflected the adaptation of congenial ideas from contemporary Christian apologists who defended theistic evolution.

Clarke began his first major theological work with the statement that "theology is preceded by religion, as botany by the life of plants. Religion is the reality of which theology is the study."[50] Again, he said: "Theology is a study, but religion is an experience. Theology is a science, but religion is a life. Theology is the study of religion and when we study theology we are studying religion."[51]

This concept, which grew out of his emphasis on the primacy of Christian experience, Clarke applied in such a way as to lead Shailer Mathews to speak of his theological system as "a religious interpretation of theology rather than a theological interpretation of religion."[52] In accord with this principle, Clarke felt that religion should determine the scope and arrangement of the materials of theology. Apologetics had a valid place in his system, but greater significance was attached to proclamation. Speculation concerning God's decrees, angels, and similar topics, which found such a prominent place in the older theologies, he dismissed as being outside the scope of religious knowledge and experience.

Clarke recognized the dynamic character of theology because he focused attention on the dynamic character of the religious life behind it. Always interested in personal and practical aspects rather than abstractions unrelated to life, he sought to set forth each significant doctrine of the Christian faith in a systematic but unscholastic manner for his own generation, confident that each succeeding generation would have the same task to perform in the light of its own experiences. It should be noted, however, that Clarke made no systematic and scientific study of the religions of the world or of the psychological aspects of the Christian religion. General observations in these realms usually stated that "it has been said for ages"[53] or "all types of Christian thinking involve it."[54] In reality, Clarke was a deeply religious man whose own personality dictated his approach to theology. Events attributed by him to universal religious experience often reflected what he felt to be true on the basis of personal experience.

Warmly evangelical[55] and vitally interested in social concerns,[56] Clarke aided many Christians of his day who felt with Harry Emerson Fosdick that they must have "new or no theology"[57] to adjust to contemporary thought patterns while retaining many of their traditional religious convictions. He was a transitional figure, however, for his views were not conservative enough for the fundamentalists nor liberal enough for the modernists in the controversy which erupted during the decade following his death.[58]

Notes

1. Walter M. Horton, "Systematic Theology" in Arnold S. Nash, ed., *Protestant Thought in the Twentieth Century* (New York: The Macmillan Co., 1951), p. 105.
2. Henry P. Van Dusen, "The Liberal Movement in Theology" in Samuel McCrea Cavert and Henry P. Van Dusen, eds., *The Church Through Half a Century* (New York: Charles Scribner's Sons, 1936), p. 68.

3. Horton, p. 105.
4. Frank Hugh Foster, *The Modern Movement in American Theology* (New York: Fleming H. Revell Co., 1939), pp. 144 f.
5. Ibid., p. 145.
6. Emily A. Clarke, ed., *William Newton Clarke: A Biography with Additional Sketches by His Friends and Colleagues* (New York: Charles Scribner's Sons, 1916), p. 41.
7. Ibid., p. 15.
8. Ibid., p. 21.
9. William Newton Clarke, *Sixty Years with the Bible* (New York: Charles Scribner's Sons, 1912), p. 35.
10. Ibid., p. 36.
11. Ibid., p. 34.
12. Ibid., p. 40.
13. Ibid., p. 202.
14. Ibid., p. 52.
15. Emily A. Clarke, p. 28.
16. Clarke, p. 63.
17. Ibid., p. 56.
18. Ibid., p. 57.
19. George Rice Hovey, *Alvah Hovey: His Life and Letters* (Philadelphia: The Judson Press, 1928), p. 155.
20. Ibid., p. 241.
21. Clarke, p. 104.
22. Ibid., p. 100.
23. Emily A. Clarke, pp. 44 f.
24. William H. Allison, "Clarke, William Newton" in *Dictionary of American Biography,* vol. iv, p. 164.
25. Clarke, pp. 116 f.
26. Ibid., p. 117.
27. Ibid., p. 116.
28. Ibid., p. 120.
29. Ibid., p. 121.
30. Allison, p. 164.
31. Emily A. Clarke, p. 145.
32. Ibid., p. 146.
33. Ibid., p. 143.
34. William Newton Clarke, *Commentary on the Gospel of Mark* (Philadelphia: American Baptist Publication Society, 1881), pp. 196-201.
35. Clarke, *Sixty Years with the Bible,* p. 170.
36. Emily A. Clarke, p. 60.
37. Clarke, *Sixty Years with the Bible,* p. 185.

38. Cited by Hovey, p. 224.
39. Harry Emerson Fosdick, *The Living of These Days: An Autobiography* (New York: Harper and Brothers Publishers, 1956), p. 55.
40. Allison, p. 164.
41. William Newton Clarke, *The Use of the Scriptures in Theology* (New York: Charles Scribner's Sons, 1906), p. 4.
42. William Newton Clarke, *An Outline of Christian Theology* (Eighteenth edition; Edinburgh, Soctland: T. and T. Clark, 1909), p. 45.
43. Clarke, *The Use of the Scriptures in Theology,* p. 62.
44. Ibid., p. 50.
45. Ibid., p. 56.
46. Ibid., p. 60.
47. Ibid., pp. 64 f.
48. Henry P. Van Dusen, "The Nineteenth Century and Today" in George F. Thomas, ed., *The Vitality of the Christian Tradition* (New York: Harper and Bros. 1941), p. 170.
49. William Newton Clarke, *Can I Believe in God the Father?* (New York: Charles Scribner's Sons, 1899), p. 50.
50. Clarke, *An Outline of Christian Theology,* p. 1.
51. William Newton Clarke, *Mystery in Religion* (Hamilton, N. Y.: Published by the Students of the Seminary, 1896), p. 4.
52. Shailer Mathews, "In Memoriam: William Newton Clarke," *The American Journal of Theology* (July 1912), p. 446.
53. William Newton Clarke, *The Christian Doctrine of God* (Edinburgh, Scotland: T. and T. Clark, 1909), p. 145.
54. Ibid., p. 169.
55. See particularly Clarke's books *A Study of Christian Missions* (New York: Charles Scribner's Sons, 1900) and *What Shall We Think of Christianity?* (4th ed.; New York: Charles Scribner's Sons, 1900).
56. Sydney Ahlstrom's contention in his article, "Theology in America," in James Ward Smith and A. Leland Jamison, eds., *The Shaping of American Religion,* (Princeton: Princeton University Press, 1961), p. 294, that Clarke lacked social concern is without foundation. He was, for example, a charter member and active participant in the Brotherhood of the Kingdom. His book, *The Ideal of Jesus* (New York: Charles Scribner's Sons, 1911) was dedicated to this organization and dealt with ethical problems.
57. Cited by Emily A. Clarke, p. 118.
58. For a systematic study of Clarke's thought see Claude L. Howe, Jr., "The Theology of William Newton Clarke" (unpublished Th.D. dissertation, New Orleans Baptist Theological Seminary, New Orleans, La., 1959).

6
Call, Placement, and Tenure
of Ministers

Baptists emphasize the priesthood of all believers, stressing that every Christian is expected to minister. Conceptually, at least, they draw no sharp distinctions between clergy and laity. Practically, however, they recognize the need for a special ministry, often defined in functional terms. In the latter sense, ministers play a significant role in Baptist life and are held in high esteem by their fellow Christians.

Concepts of church and ministry are intertwined. T. W. Manson argued cogently that "there is only one 'essential ministry' in the Church, the perpetual ministry of the risen and ever-present Lord himself."[1] In this view, the church is a minister, continuing the ministry of Christ. "Thus all Christians stand on common ground, and all participate in the continuing ministry of the living Lord as his body, the church. There are different ministries among Christians, but all are ministers."[2]

The vast diversity of ministries today is recognized and appreciated, as is the fact that every ministry begins with an activity of God. Most comments that follow, however, relate rather specifically to pastoral ministry in and through Baptist churches. Special attention is given to the dynamics of communicating, authenticating, and actuating the call of God to the gospel ministry.

The Call to the Ministry

H. Richard Niebuhr noted that whenever there has been a definite, intelligible conception of the ministry in Christian history, at least four things were known. These included the chief work or purpose of ministry, what constitutes a call to the ministry, the source of authority for the minister, and whom the minister serves.[3] All of these are obviously important, but our concern at the moment is with the matter of call. Here Niebuhr asserts that a call to the ministry includes at least the following four elements:

(1) *the call to be a Christian,* which is variously described as the call to discipleship of Jesus Christ, to hearing and doing of the Word of God, to repentance and faith, et cetera;
(2) *the secret call,* namely, that inner persuasion or experience whereby a person feels himself directly summoned or invited by God to take up the work of the ministry;
(3) *the providential call,* which is that invitation and command to assume the work of the ministry which comes through the equipment of a person with the talents necessary for the exercise of the office and through the divine guidance of his life by all its circumstances;
(4) *the ecclesiastical call,* that is, the summons and invitation extended to a man by some community or institution of the Church to engage in the work of the ministry.[4]

The above elements are virtually always present to some extent, but conflict and confusion have occurred often with respect to their relative importance and proper relationships.

The call to be a Christian is primary and prerequisite for ministry. "At no time have the Church and the churches not required of candidates for the ministry that they be first of all men of Christian conviction, however such conviction and its guarantees were interpreted."[5] For Baptists, membership in the church is restricted to those who have professed repentance toward God and faith in the Lord Jesus Christ. Virtually every candidate for ordination is questioned regarding his "conversion experience." The issue is not the significance of the Christian call but the sufficiency of it. Is there a call to special ministry besides or beyond the call to be a Christian? If so, how does it differ from the call to discipleship that is so prominent in Scripture?

J. Winston Pearce published the study course book *God Calls Me* in 1958. It was used extensively in Southern Baptist churches. "*Every* Christian should be called of God to the work in which he is engaged, not just the person engaged in some church-related task," Pearce contended. "That is in no sense an effort to discredit the significance of God's call to church work; it is, rather, to lift all vocations up to its lofty level."[6] Pearce did not deny that God calls individuals to church-related vocations, but neither did he distinguish this call in any distinctive sense from a call to another vocation.

Two years later Franklin M. Segler *(A Theology of Church and Ministry)* continued to stress Christian vocation in general, citing concepts of Martin Luther and others. "It is not valid to consider the gospel ministry as the only vocation into which men are called by God to serve their generation."[7] Segler contended, however, that Christian ministry is "a unique vocation," citing the Bible and church history in support of the idea of a special call.[8] "Two things, then, make it logical that God has a special call to the ministry: representatives are needed to proclaim God's Word, which is a special revelation, and to serve God's church, which is a special institution. The world needs to be reminded of the supernatural through a unique witness."[9]

These matters were explored much more fully by Henlee H. Barnette in *Christian Calling and Vocation* (1965). "So central is the concept of calling in the Bible that it becomes the integrating symbol of the Christian life."[10] Barnette argued that calling today has lost its biblical content, describing, on the one hand, one's occupation or profession or, on the other hand, those appointed to engage in full-time Christian service. "There is but one call in the Scriptures, to be a child of God and to behave as such."[11] Christians are thus summoned to participate in the eternal purpose and plan of God.

God's aim is to reconcile all things in Christ. The gospel is the good news that God works for the redemption of the whole universe, that all things are to be united in Christ, and that each Christian has his own proper role to play in the accomplishment of this great goal (I Corinthians 12; Ephesians 4:1ff). Calling is the religious symbol by which this whole experience is described and communicated to man.[12]

Barnette argued that the distinction between sacred and secular callings should be abolished, and every Christian should consider himself a minister of the gospel. But within the general calling, there are particular callings to various ministries, differentiated by a variety of gifts provided by the Spirit for the benefit of the church. "Within the universal and primary call of God there are those who serve in special religious functions as pastor, apostle, teacher, and so forth, according to their gifts and competence. But this does not make them superior to the church or to their fellow Christians."[13]

A more recent discussion of calling that gives primacy to the Christian call is found in *The Greening of the Church* by Findley B. Edge. Edge argues that the work of the church is being done by the wrong people in the wrong place. Stressing the priesthood of all believers, he states that *"the call to salvation and the call to the ministry is one and the same call. That is, when one is called by God to be a part of his people, he is also called into the ministry."*[14] God has called the laity to be his basic ministers. At the same time, he has called others for special ministry, namely an equipping ministry (Eph. 4:11-12), in which they serve as "player-coaches."[15] What is God's basic call? "It is a call to mission. A mission that is redemptive in nature. This redemption is personal and social. It is a call to ministry. Each individual is to fulfill God's mission through his own ministry. The call to be a part of God's people and the call to ministry are one and the same."[16]

None of the persons cited above would deny that God calls individuals for leadership functions in the churches, but, with the exception of Segler, their primary emphasis is upon the Christian call. They are representative of numerous others who have spoken or written in a similar manner. But for the pastoral ministry, especially, the vast majority of Baptists still emphasize a secret call that is in some sense unique. As a matter of fact, until recent decades one who spoke of a call in Baptist life was regarded as destined for service as a pastor or missionary.

John Calvin recognized a secret call, "of which every minister is conscious to himself before God, but which is not known to the Church."[17] Baptists have normally expected that such a call be made known to the church, for candidates for ordination are virtually always questioned regarding their call. The concern is not how the call came, whether in a cataclysmic experience or as a growing conviction, but that the individual possesses an inner conviction that God has summoned him personally for the ministry of the gospel. T. A. Patterson, for example, has insisted that there is a difference between the call to preach and the call to enter another field of service. "Those who insist that there is no difference simply reveal one thing," he said, "they have never been called to preach."[18]

Duke McCall likewise argues for a clear distinction. "Without disparaging the role or ministry of the laity," he said, "the church has always held that it was a special act of divine providence which provided the church with its representative Ministry."[19] McCall contended that a watered-down conviction concerning the miracle of conversion leads inevitably to a watered-down conception of the call to the gospel ministry.

Let individual pastors become God's prophets who insist that no one becomes a part of the local church until there is a genuine miraculous conversion of a sinner into a child of God. Let these same individual pastors begin to say not only that God has called every Christian to a ministry of Christian faith and witness, but also that God has called some, by a miraculous experience, into the Ministry of the gospel.[20]

The personal nature and meaning of such a call is reflected by many others. "I believe that every Christian has a vocation, a calling under God," declared Ted Adams. "I believe, however, that in church-related work there is a special sense of call beyond the influence of any human factor."[21] Adams reflected upon his own experience, which is highly representative. "I remember when I felt called to the ministry. It was as clear to me as any experience in my life, and I have never doubted it since. Nor would I take anything in exchange for the sense of call and its dedication."[22] Herschel Hobbs likewise acknowledged that God extends a call for service to every Christian and decried a sharp division between clergy and laity. But one extreme had been replaced by another. "Hence, today the attitude is widespread that God calls all Christians on the same basis," Hobbs said. "This serves to diminish the idea of a divine call being given to certain Christians for specific spiritual services, as over against other honored and useful vocations."[23] After citing a number of Scripture passages, Hobbs stated his conclusion that "the Scriptures teach the fact of a divine call given by God to specific persons for specific purposes. This does not diminish the sanctity of any vocation dedicated to God's will. But it does enhance the calling of those who are chosen of God for services of a peculiarly spiritual nature."[24]

Thus far it is evident that Baptists who desire to lift up the calling of the laity stress the Christian call while those who would enhance the calling to special service emphasize the secret call. Less attention has been given by Baptists to the providential call. They assume that the God who calls provides the necessary talents and opportunities, though the individual may not develop or utilize them. Baptist churches are more hesitant today than in the past to encourage those with evident capabilities to consider special ministry in the church, and they are likewise hesitant to discourage those who appear to lack certain abilities if these affirm that God has called them for a particular ministry.

These remarks have obvious implications for "calling out the called." In the Baptist heritage, an individual who professed a call to the gospel ministry might be granted the privilege by the church to "exercise his gifts" before the church or in surrounding areas. The privilege might be extended or restricted in various ways. In this manner, the church could assess the validity of the call and the qualifications of the individual in relation to it. On the other hand, a church might take the initiative and encourage a capable member in this direction.

The experience of John Mason Peck with the Durham Church in 1811 is typical of what is being described. "On our first acquaintance with the members of this church, even before receiving baptism, nearly every male member had had conversation with us on what appeared to the writer a momentous question," Peck recalled. " 'Don't you think you ought to preach the gospel?' was seriously asked in every instance of private conversation. The pastor, in particular, was too inquisitive to permit an evasive answer."[25] Peck admitted that he had already been struggling with this question. The struggle continued for some months after his baptism, and Peck was urged to disclose his feelings to the brotherhood. After this was done, the church voted for him to improve his gifts, including conducting the meeting the next afternoon. In about three months, the limits were extended to neighboring churches and finally to "wherever Divine Providence might open the door."[26]

Baptists in general and Southern Baptists in particular usually have avoided establishing specific requirements, educational or otherwise, for service as ministers. Rapid growth on the frontier resulted partly from the ability to provide ministers, often limited in talent and training, to establish and lead churches. Other seminary professors could join me in recalling numerous surprises over the past two decades when God has blessed the ministry of individuals who, during their time in seminary, appeared lacking in many of the desired characteristics or capabilities. Southern Baptists from the beginning have maintained virtually an open-door policy in their seminaries and have sought to provide courses of study for students with varied academic backgrounds.

God calls ministers, but churches also call ministers. The relationship between the two calls is not always clear. Ideally, the church has the power directly from Christ and under his lordship to select its leaders and order its affairs. A vote represents an effort to discern the will of Christ regarding any matter under consideration, including the selection of ministers. A church seeks a God-called minister and affirms through a call its belief that God desires the minister to serve in and through that church. The minister in turn examines his own call and accepts or rejects the invitation of the church. Human limitations operate at every level, and conclusions of the church and minister may differ. The relationship is not established unless both respond affirmatively. Processes behind what had been described will be discussed at another point, but it is clear from what has been said that the ecclesiastical call is most significant in Baptist life and operates principally at the local level. Associations, conventions, and institutions recognize that this is a very sensitive area in Baptist life and become involved, if at all, only in assisting churches and ministers to become acquainted one with the other.

Placement and Tenure in the Ministry

How do Baptist churches establish, maintain, and terminate pastoral relationships? The correct answer might be "with great difficulty." There are many instances where a person responds to the call to be Christian, professes a special call from God to the gospel ministry, provides some evidence of providential leading by native endowment and academic training, but for some reason is unable to secure a call from a church, agency, or institution. A Doctor of Ministry project at the New Orleans Baptist Theological Seminary in 1977 focused upon needs of "inexperienced preachers" (who professed a call of God to preach but had not been called by a church) in one Alabama association with sixty-four churches.[27] The associational annual listed seventy-two such individuals. If this association is anywhere near representative, then "many are called but few are chosen."[28]

Churches at the present time experience less difficulty in securing pastors. Approximately 10 percent of the churches in the Southern Baptist Convention are without pastors, but most of these have ample recommendations and are evaluating potential candidates. More serious is the number of churches with pastors who desire to relocate. The problem of placement has been described as "the most crucial question facing Southern Baptist ministers."[29] Following a brief discussion of how Baptist churches in the past secured their pastors, attention will be focused upon the contemporary situation, particularly with respect to the role of local churches, seminaries, and conventions or associations.

For many decades, Baptist churches more often than not selected a pastor from among the membership. John Taylor described the process at Clear Creek, Kentucky, with Lewis Craig serving as moderator (1785).

His mode was to ask every member of the church, male or female, bound or free, who do you choose for your pastor—I think the church was now about sixty in number. I must confess it filled me with surprise, when the first man that was asked answered that he chose me; and my astonishment continued to increase until the question went all around, only one man objected, but Lewis Craig soon worked him out of his objection, for it lay in thinking my coat was too fine. For my own part, I did think that no man in the church had the mind of Christ but this objector.[30]

Edward J. Hiscox commented regarding the process in 1894. "Primarily and properly, though not necessarily, the pastor is chosen from among the members, after the Church has had evidence that the Spirit had called to, and fitted him for, the work of the ministry; and after having abundant evidence of his adaptation to the position."[31]

On numerous occasions, of course, churches needed or desired to search outside the present membership. Especially when ministers were scarce, a church might request an individual or group to communicate with those who might assist in the matter. During the Colonial period, for example, churches often wrote Baptist groups in England or the Philadelphia Association describing their circumstances and needs. Such correspondence brought Abel Morgan and Morgan Edwards from England to Philadelphia and Oliver Hart from the Philadelphia area to Charleston. A component largely missing from Baptist life today was that if the pastor of another church was approached, that church was brought into the negotiations.

As the number of available pastors increased and as educational and professional backgrounds became more important, churches surveyed a larger group of potential candidates when seeking a pastor. This was done in a variety of ways, but most often a committee of some sort was given the responsibility for locating and screening prospects. The First

Baptist Church of Nashville, for example, appointed a pulpit committee of three in 1834. "The church directed them to correspond with any minister they considered to be a worthy candidate. They were to invite him to visit Nashville and confer with the church on the subject of a call."[32] This same church appointed the deacons as a pulpit committee in 1870[33] and "all adult male members" for the same purpose in 1889.[34] Four years later a committee consisted of twenty-six men and fifteen women, the latter being included for the first time.[35]

The normal procedure is somewhat more uniform today, but basic essentials have not changed. A church seeking a pastor usually chooses a pastor selection committee. The committee identifies, screens, and confers with prospects, finally recommending a particular individual for consideration by the church. This individual visits the church and leads the congregation in worship. At an announced time the church votes upon the recommendation of the committee.

Within the simple process described are many variations. The size, composition, resources, authority, and procedures of such a committee are not fixed, even when the committee approach is used. A committee is not always representative of the membership, even though elected by the congregation. Some committees agree in advance upon procedures, qualifications desired, and so forth, while others simply begin visiting prospects that are recommended. Guidelines provided by pamphlets, such as *The Pastor Selection Committee* or Ernest Mosley in *Called to Joy,* may be used, modified, or ignored. Mosley is correct in stating that "a study of practices followed by Southern Baptist churches in finding, calling, inducting, and orienting pastoral ministries leaders would surely reveal a strange assortment of practices."[36] One item that does not vary, however, is the authority of the total congregation in the final decision. A committee may select, negotiate with, and recommend a pastoral candidate, but the formal call is extended by the church itself.

Seminaries exercise a limited role in assisting churches to secure pastors (and other ministers), or, more accurately, pastors to secure churches. Each seminary maintains a placement service (by whatever name) for currently enrolled students, graduating seniors, and alumni. Many churches in the immediate geographical area of a seminary use student pastors regularly. The seminary provides several biographical resumés for a pastor selection committee and arranges an interview if requested, but the initiative from that point is with the committee and church.

Seminary placement personnel also receive requests from churches throughout the nation who are interested in calling a graduating senior. Here again, the seminary provides several biographical resumés of potential candidates and cooperates as requested in assisting candidates and churches to become acquainted. At New Orleans in 1978, for example, 154 students with interest in pastoral work were graduated, and 143 requests from churches were received. Requests for music and education ministers, on the other hand, far exceeded the number of graduates in these areas. From a total of 298 graduates in all categories during May and December of 1978, however, 230 have secured places of service.

Seminaries are less successful in assisting alumni, especially pastors, to relocate. Individual seminary professors, of course, are contacted by pastors desiring to relocate and by churches seeking pastors. Also, alumni often inform seminary placement personnel concerning their needs or desires; but the results are usually disappointing. The presence of the personal ingredient, wherein the individual making a recommen-dation knows and is known by the pastor selection committee as well as the candidate, is undoubtedly a significant factor in securing considera-tion. This is especially true since a latent suspicion that something must be wrong with a pastor desiring to relocate often must be overcome.

State conventions have become more actively and openly involved in assisting pastors and churches in finding one another during the last decade. Prior to that time assistance was on an informal and largely individual basis, but now almost half the conventions maintain an office of church-minister relations (by various names). The North Carolina Bap-tist Convention began such a service in 1964 because one-third of the correspondence to the executive secretary came from pastors desiring to relocate. The Georgia Baptist Convention authorized a service in 1970, electing a full-time secretary the following year. A dozen others (Alabama, Florida, Illinois, Kentucky, Louisiana, Mississippi, Missouri, Oklahoma, South Carolina, Tennessee, Texas, and Virginia) have estab-lished an office for this purpose. In conventions where a formal structure does not exist, the responsibility is borne by the executive secretary or the director of missions.

The following comments are based upon an analysis of materials provided by twenty-seven state conventions. First, the conventions avoid use of the word *placement* and deny that they serve as *placement bureaus.* They provide information upon request about churches and pastors, usually without evaluation or recommendation. A church may request resumés of prospective pastors or information about a particular pastor. In the former case, several resumés are shared; and in the latter, biographical information on file or provided by the pastor is sent. Further investigation is left to the parties directly involved in the negotiations.

Second, the process of gathering and maintaining information about churches and pastors is strictly on a voluntary basis. Most conventions have formulated questionnaires for this purpose; no church or pastor is pressured to provide information, and each may specify circumstances under which the information is to be shared. The questionnaires themselves vary from convention to convention. All request the usual biographical information from pastors regarding education, experience, and so forth. Most include questions regarding cooperation with and support of the denomination. Several inquire about doctrinal matters, ranging from views about the Bible and theology to practices in administering the ordinances. Some include questions about personal health or habits, such as smoking. Information requested from churches is less detailed including matters, such as size and budget, positions to be filled, salaries provided, personal qualities desired, and special needs or requirements.

Third, convention personnel cooperate closely with area missionaries within the convention, receiving and supplying information that is current. They also contact and visit seminaries and colleges, securing information about individuals interested in serving in a particular area. In these and other ways, they seek to extend the supply of prospects while remaining sensitive to local needs and conditions.

Finally, a number of the conventions have extended their range of services to include counseling, conferences, writing and/or distributing literature, and conducting studies of such matters as salaries and tenure.

Pastor support services of various kinds will no doubt increase as the conventions mature in identifying needs and providing assistance in church-minister relations.

Few studies of pastoral tenure have been made, and most of these are somewhat superficial and inconclusive. A study in Virginia in 1977 indicated an increase in pastoral tenure to 6.71 years from a 4 year tenure in 1973. The increase was attributed to the following primary factors:

1. More churches are providing reasonably adequate income.
2. High incidence of pastors' wives secularly employed tends to deter mobility . . . .
3. Some churches are discovering that changing pastors does not automatically solve a church's problems.
4. Some pastors are "locked" into situations by their inability to relocate.
5. Longer tenure in some churches indicates health in the church-minister relationship.
6. Movement of pastors over 50 years of age is increasingly difficult.

Heavy attrition occurred between years two and three, five and seven, and twelve and fifteen. "This supports the generalization that the church-minister relationship tends to experience periods of high stress leading to separation at those times."[37]

Tenure reported by other conventions was much less. Kentucky estimated pastoral tenure at four years,[38] Alabama at thirty months,[39] and North Carolina at twenty-two months.[40] A. B. Colvin of Kentucky observed that "inability of pastors and other ministers to lead their people into personal ministries is the outstanding cause of short tenure."[41] Sam Granade of Alabama reported that the question of rapid turnover was discussed in detail in a seminar-type setting with participants concluding that the following factors were prominent causes: (1) inadequate salary and allowance; (2) inadequate process of calling a pastor; (3) lack of support programs for pastor; (4) low image of pastorate and total mission programs; and (5) inadequate understanding of roles.[42] Robert Bruhn of North Carolina noted that student pastorates and inability of smaller churches to provide financially for pastors with growing families decreased tenure.[43]

A "Ministerial Attrition Study" by the Research Services Department of The Baptist Sunday School Board concluded that "the majority of those who resign from church staff positions do so for very understandable reasons, i.e., retirement, health, to further their education, to enter another type of church-related vocation, et cetera. The survey surfaced very little discontent and disenchantment with the ministry."[44] This conclusion, however, is based upon the assumption that, of those not seeking another church staff position, the 25.9 percent who resigned for "personal reasons" should not be interpreted as "unhappy with the ministry." Recent observations by Porter Routh provide an additional perspective for the matter under discussion. "I am convinced," he said, "after being associated with ministers all of my life and working closely with them for more than thirty years, that the biggest problem they face is phoniness."[45] By phoniness he meant identity crisis or role confusion.

Some studies that have recently been made of Southern Baptist ministers reflect something of the results of this unclear sense of direction. I do not know that it is any worse than it has been. The dropout rate stays at about 3% a year. One study of seminary students showed that about 17% doubted they would choose the ministry if they were college freshmen again. A study made by Mr. Gallup shows that 32% of all Protestant ministers have considered leaving their religious vocation. The major reasons are inability to communicate and finances. About one-third of all SBC pastors move each year, and the average tenure is about two and one-half years. There seems to be a growing sense on the part of many ministers of an inadequate support system. This not only reflects the sour smell of poverty (Southern Baptist ministers rank seventeenth among the top twenty denominations) but also the need for more adequate counseling both for personal problems and church problems. There has been a shift in the image of the minister from pastor-preacher to administrator-counselor. One study by Sam Blizzard showed more than 70% of the time of the full-time urban pastor was taken in administration and counseling, and many ministers feel their training does not prepare them for this reality.[46]

The fact that on the average Southern Baptist pastors change churches every thirty months and that a substantial portion at any one time desire to relocate indicates the critical nature of church-minister relations in Baptist life.

At the present time Southern Baptist churches suffer somewhat because of the brief tenure of their pastors, but pastors suffer much more because of problems in placement. The problem of securing initial placement has not yet reached the critical stage, but relocation for many is virtually impossible. As the age of the pastor increases above fifty, or as special difficulties arise, pastors are forced into secular jobs or locked into positions that are insecure or unchallenging. The time has come for Southern Baptists to admit that a serious problem exists in this area which demands detailed study and creative action.

Evaluative Reflections and Suggestions

Baptists are not alone in problems relating to call, placement, and tenure of ministers. Few Baptists would exchange their approach to these matters with other groups. But this fact provides little comfort for pastors and churches penalized by the approach and less justification for ignoring problems that obviously exist. The solution is not to adopt an episcopal or presbyterian polity but to inject procedures and safeguards into the congregational polity of Baptists designed to produce healthier churches and happier ministers. Reflections and/or suggestions that follow are based upon this central conviction.

With respect to call, this study has affirmed anew that Southern Baptists believe in a God-called ministry. They are convinced that God chooses individuals for unique service in and through the church. For most, however, the conception of call is highly individualized, regarded primarily as an experience between God and the individual. The public profession of call may be shared in a service of worship, but the initiative is normally with the one called. Nor are Christian commitment and providential ability examined closely by the community of believers. Preparation for ministry may be anticipated but is not required. A subsequent call by a church may indicate a place of service but is not regarded as essential for a call to service. Consideration should be given to strengthening the role of representative segments of the Christian community in assisting those whom God calls to respond to, prepare for, and engage in their calling. Apparently far more individuals profess a call from God than actually pursue their calling. Additional guidance and support from the local church, association, state convention, and the Southern Baptist Convention might conceivably reduce this disparity and provide personnel to carry the gospel to every creature as envisioned in Bold Mission Thrust.

The local church should become more active not only in calling out the called but also in nurturing, clarifying, and evaluating gifts of the called in light of the person's abilities, the church's mission, and the world's needs. The association could provide opportunities for authenticating the call, counsel and discussion regarding implications of a call, and fellowship among the called. State conventions could design more extensive and effective programs of vocational guidance utilizing the expertise of competent teachers, church leaders, and denominational representatives. The Southern Baptist Convention could establish guidelines, formulate principles, provide literature, and train leadership to assist the called in making vocational choices, securing training, and engaging in ministry.

Southern Baptists believe also in a God-placed ministry. A church without a minister prays that God will lead to the person divinely prepared for the position. A minister without a church or desiring another church prays for divine guidance and assistance. But since God more often than not works through human instruments, the process is often shortcircuited.

One source of ministerial frustration is that churches exercise a freedom of initiative and investigation normally denied a minister. Seldom does a minister desiring to relocate approach pastor selection committees directly, providing qualifications and references. Pastor selection committees, on the other hand, determine qualifications, list prospects, and approach individuals freely. Mutual freedom might be allowed without rejecting a sense of divine leadership.

Perhaps the greatest need today in terms of placement, however, is for a redistribution of personnel. God continues to call and individuals respond, but the result is an overabundance of ministers in areas where demands are least. Pioneer areas and mission boards recruit with meager responses, and educational and music positions in many churches remain unstaffed.

The most promising development designed to deal with a multiplicity of problems is efforts by the state conventions to establish offices of church-minister relations. Such offices, cooperating with associational personnel, could become effective channels for vocational guidance, personal and career counseling, and studies regarding salary and tenure. When fully accepted and trusted, they will be able to provide placement information and recommendations without infringing upon the rights of churches or ministers. Cooperating with other state conventions and Southern Baptist Convention agencies, they could maintain central pools of information regarding crucial needs and available personnel. Working with colleges and seminaries, they could identify rights and responsibilities of churches and ministers, support continuing education, and clarify identity roles and crisis producing factors.[47]

Finally, Southern Baptists believe in a God-tenured ministry. Ministers and churches affirm the leadership of God in establishing relationships. But God apparently changes his mind in about thirty months, if tenure is any indication. Perhaps churches and ministers should consider seriously entering into a mutual covenant with one another involving a minimum time period. Also, a church seeking an established minister should be sensitive to needs and desires of the sister church, requesting that church also to seek God's leadership in the decision. More important, however, churches and/or ministers facing problems should seek together to work through those problems and toward goals meaningful for the ministry of both. When the relationship is severed, minister and church should manifest the spirit of Christ, taking action that would best preserve the usefulness of the minister and the witness of the church. Avoiding radical individualism and autocratic ecclesiasticism, Southern Baptist churches and ministers face the challenge of strengthening the body of Christ and boldly sharing the gospel of reconciliation in one of the most exciting periods of Christian history.

Notes

1. T. W. Manson, *The Church's Ministry* (Philadelphia: The Westminster Press, 1948), p. 107.
2. Frank Stagg, *New Testament Theology* (Nashville: Broadman Press, 1962), p. 253.
3. H. Richard Niebuhr, *The Purpose of the Church and Its Ministry* (New York: Harper and Row, Publishers, 1956), p. 58.
4. Ibid., p. 64. The Baptist historian Morgan Edwards cited essentially the same elements in 1768. See his *Customs of the Primitive Churches* (Philadelphia, 1768), pp. 13 *ff.*

5.   Niebuhr, p. 64.
6.   J. Winston Pearce, *God Calls Me* (Nashville: Convention Press, 1958), p. 47.
7.   Franklin M. Segler, *A Theology of Church and Ministry* (Nashville: Broadman Press, 1960), p. 39.
8.   Ibid., p. 40.
9.   Ibid., p. 42.
10. Henlee H. Barnette, *Christian Calling and Vocation* (Grand Rapids: Baker Book House, 1965), p. 12.
11. Ibid., p. 79.
12. Ibid., p. 21. Cf. W. O. Carver, *The Glory of God in the Christian Calling* (Nashville: Broadman Press, 1949).
13. Barnette, p. 79.
14. Findley B. Edge, *The Greening of the Church* (Waco: Word Books, Publishers, 1971), p. 38.
15. Ibid., p. 43. Cf. Elton Trueblood, *The Company of the Committed* (New York: Harper and Row, 1961).
16. Edge, p. 47. See also Albert L. Meiburg, *Called to Minister* (Nashville: Convention Press, 1968).
17. Hugh Thomson Kerr, Jr., *A Compend of the Institutes of the Christian Religion by John Calvin* (Philadelphia: Presbyterian Board of Christian Education, 1939), p. 166.
18. *Baptist Standard,* October 4, 1961, p. 2.
19. *The Tie,* May 1965, p. 2.
20. Ibid.
21. Theodore F. Adams, "Inside a Baptist Church," in *A Way Home,* James Saxon Childers, ed. (Atlanta: Tupper and Love, Inc., 1964), p. 190.
22. Ibid.
23. Herschel H. Hobbs, "The Pastor's Calling," in *Baker's Dictionary of Practical Theology,* ed. Ralph G. Turnbull (Grand Rapids: Baker Book House, 1967), p. 292.
24. Ibid. Cf. also James Hardee Kennedy, *The Commission of Moses and the Christian Calling* (Grand Rapids: Wm. B. Eerdman's Publishing Company, 1964).
25. *Memoir of John Mason Peck* (Edited by Rufus Babcock. Introduction by Paul M. Harrison. Carbondale, Illinois: Southern Illinois University Press, 1965), p. 26.
26. Ibid., p. 28.
27. William L. Hacker, Jr., "A Program of Vocational Guidance for Inexperienced Preachers in the Morgan County Baptist Association, Alabama" (D.Min. Project Report, New Orleans Baptist Theological Seminary, 1977).

28. Matt. 22:14. Cf. Everett B. Barnard, "God's Call and Its Relationship to Career Changes." *Search* 7 (Fall 1976): 9-15.
29. E. B. Bratcher, "An Overview of the Personal and Vocational Needs of Ministers." *Search* 8 (Fall 1976):24.
30. William Warren Sweet, *Religion on the American Frontier: The Baptists 1783-1830* (New York: Cooper Square Publishers, Inc., 1964), p. 153. See Bratcher, pp. 39 *ff.* for an excellent description of how frontier Baptist churches "raised up" their preachers.
31. Edward H. Hiscox, *The New Directory of Baptist Churches* (Philadelphia: American Baptist Publication Society, 1894), p. 99.
32. Lynn E. May, Jr., *The First Baptist Church of Nashville, Tennessee, 1820-1970* (Nashville: First Baptist Church, 1970), p. 45.
33. Ibid., p. 134.
34. Ibid., p. 159.
35. Ibid., p. 163.
36. Ernest E. Mosley, *Called to Joy* (Nashville: Convention Press, 1973), p. 34.
37. "Pastoral Tenure in Virginia Baptist Churches" (unpublished study furnished by James C. Massey, Director of Church-Ministry Relations).
38. A. B. Colvin, personal letter.
39. Sam Granade, personal letter.
40. Robert H. Bruhn, personal letter.
41. Colvin.
42. Granade.
43. Bruhn.
44. Kenneth E. Hayes, "Ministerial Attrition Study" (unpublished study, September, 1977), p. 3.
45. Porter Routh, "Preparation of Ministers Competent to Minister." *Theological Education* XV No. 2 (Spring 1979), p. 103.
46. Ibid.
47. A most helpful analysis of this matter has been provided by Albert McClellan, "Providing a Support System for Ministers" *Search* 7 (Fall 1976): 42-49.

7
Christian Ordinances in Baptist Churches

Introduction

Writing this chapter dealing with Christian ordinances in Baptist churches provided an opportunity for reflection on my own religious heritage and personal experience. The term *ordinances* itself is part of that heritage and experience, for Baptists in America prefer *ordinances* rather than *sacraments*. Neither term has a biblical basis but the latter, in the understanding of many, carries the idea of *ex opere operato,* or that God's grace is dispensed almost automatically through participation in the observance. The central emphasis of the former term is understood to be upon obedience so that the participant is doing that which Christ explicitly instituted and commanded.

The 1963 "Baptist Faith and Message" expands the 1925 statement which it follows at several points, one of which describes each ordinance as an "act of obedience." Baptists believe that in observing the ordinances they are carrying out the commands of Jesus Christ. The 1963 statement likewise specifies the ordinances as "two" in number, whereas, the earlier statement refers simply to the "ordinances of Christ," but the change is not substantive. The "sacraments" varied in number for over a thousand years, but Peter Lombard in his *Sentences* (c. 1150) defended seven, namely, baptism, the Lord's Supper, confirmation, penance, extreme unction, ordination, and matrimony. Martin Luther challenged the last five from a biblical perspective. Most Protestants, including Baptists, have accepted only the first two as Christian ordinances instituted by Christ. Some Baptists have practiced foot-washing and the laying on of hands, but these have not been placed on a level of equality with baptism and the Lord's Supper. Christ exhorted his followers to baptize (Matt. 28:19-20) and share the bread and wine "in remembrance of me" (1 Cor. 11:24-25). These commands have been interpreted as directed to all believers in all ages. Christ instituted two and only two ordinances, which are to be observed as he commanded until he returns.

Personal Recollections

Although more years have passed than I care to admit, I recall vividly my own baptism. After a week of revival preaching, the baptismal service was scheduled for Saturday morning at Giles pool in the open countryside. A large congregation gathered for the occasion, including animals. At the appropriate time, the animals were herded from the pool. The congregation prayed and sang and listened to a brief sermon followed by an invitation for others to trust Christ and follow him in baptism. Then the minister of the small church in the nearby village, who happened to be my father, entered the water followed by a band of recent converts. Each candidate had previously made a public profession of faith in Christ and expressed a desire to be baptized and unite with the church. One by one the converts were immersed in water in the name of the Father, Son, and Holy Spirit. For some, this appeared to be a solemn occasion. For others, who were presumed to be less "spiritual," it was an occasion for laughter and chatter as the water splashed or the animals moved.

The minister, who had five or six years earlier experienced a profound spiritual change in a semi-pentecostal service under a brush arbor, conducted the observance in an orderly fashion befitting the occasion. I reflect even today with some surprise that among the converts baptized that morning were two future preachers and several dedicated laypersons who would be stabilizing forces in Baptist churches for many decades.

The *mode* of baptism was important and impressive. It was important enough for this congregation to gather at an inconvenient time and place and impressive enough that I recall many of the details. But the *meaning* of the observance was not obscured. Even at age eleven, I was aware that a change had taken place in my life by trusting Christ. In baptism, I was not only obeying him but also portraying the essential elements of the gospel, the death, burial, and resurrection of Christ. My resolve that day, though broken many times in years to come, was to walk in newness of life made possible in Christ.

A quarter-century later I had the privilege of baptizing my son. The setting was quite different: during morning worship, in a "high church" atmosphere at St. Charles Avenue Baptist Church, in New Orleans. But many elements were the same: a Christian congregation prayed and sang; the word was preached and an invitation extended; professed believers were immersed in water in the name of the Father, Son, and Holy Spirit. In contrast, I have no clear recollection of participating at an early age in observing the Lord's Supper. First communion is significant and remembered by many Christians, but Baptist youngsters partake routinely after baptism. I do recall being taught, however, that participation at the Lord's table should follow baptism and be confined to Baptist churches. Most of the churches with which I was associated observed the ordinance quarterly at the close of a regular service of worship. The observance was often hurried, but bread and grape juice were distributed to all Baptists present. The congregation was reminded of the broken body and shed blood of Christ and was encouraged to examine themselves and to partake of the elements memorializing the death of Christ and anticipating his second coming.

Historical Issues

Baptists throughout their history have debated a number of issues related to the ordinances with other Christians and among themselves. Since baptism is the more distinctive ordinance, most discussions with other Christians have involved, directly or indirectly, this ordinance.

Is baptism for infants or believers? Baptists have insisted consistently that it is for professed believers *only*. John Smyth argued in 1609 that there is neither precept nor example for infant baptism in the New Testament and that Christ commanded his followers to make disciples and then to baptize them. The name "Anabaptists" or "re-baptizers" was attached to those who rejected infant baptism. Baptists responded that they were not "re-baptizing" since infant baptism was not valid. They refused also to equate New Testament baptism with Old Testament circumcision.

In insisting upon baptism for believers only, Baptists constituted a small minority, for most Christians continued baptizing infants. In the nineteenth and twentieth centuries, a few small groups emerged that rejected infant baptism, but until that time only Baptists and Anabaptists (Mennonites and similar groups) insisted upon baptism for professed believers. Studies by well-known non-Baptists, such as Karl Barth and others in recent decades, have strengthened the Baptist position theologically and psychologically but have brought no radical changes in practice among other Christian groups.[1] Strangely, however, while others are at least admitting the defensibility of believers' baptism, some Baptists, especially in England, are indicating a willingness to accept infant baptism.[2]

Within Baptist churches the issue of the proper candidate for baptism has focused more on practical rather than on theoretical matters. The age at which children profess conversion and request baptism has decreased substantially, and it is not unusual for those five or six years of age, or even younger, to be baptized. Ministers approach the matter cautiously, hesitating to affirm that a child reared in a Christian home cannot make an intelligent commitment at an early age. At least one Baptist pastor has suggested a change in theology to undergird the practice, but the suggestion has been largely ignored.[3]

Another practical problem has involved whether mature Christians baptized as infants should be accepted as members in Baptist churches without baptizing them as believers. Many churches in the North have followed this practice, as have a few in the South. Although not without precedent in Baptist history from the seventeenth century, this practice appears to compromise traditional Baptist convictions regarding baptism and the church. "A Baptist church, by its presentation of Believers' Baptism, claims more emphatically than any other to be built up of convinced men," declared H. Wheeler Robinson. "This ideal it stands for, and offers as its characteristic contribution to the religious life of the world."[4]

Is baptism by sprinkling or immersion? Most biblical commentators and historians agree that baptism as depicted in the New Testament was by immersion. This mode predominated for many centuries in the Western church and continues today in Eastern Orthodoxy. The central issue for Baptists in England early in the seventeenth century was believers' baptism, but the mode by immersion began to be emphasized around 1640. The First London Confession in 1644 required believers' baptism *by immersion*. The distinctive emphasis has not been that baptism by immersion is valid, which all Christian groups would accept, but that *only* baptism by immersion is valid. Biblical evidence (*baptizo*, and so forth) and the appropriate symbolism for death, burial, and resurrection are major consideration in this affirmation. "Christian baptism is the immersion of a believer in water in the name of the Father, the Son, and the Holy Spirit."[5] Virtually every Baptist confession has contained the essence of this 1963 statement regarding baptism.

Not until the nineteenth century did Baptists broaden their interest to any great extent from the candidate and mode of baptism to include the administrator and intent. Few Baptist churches until that time had faced the problem of "alien immersion," that is, immersion of a believer by a non-Baptist, and these had responded in a variety of ways. As other groups, especially the Disciples movement, adopted the immersion of adults while seemingly compromising believers' baptism by regarding baptism as an essential step in salvation, the problem became more crucial for Baptists. J. R. Graves declared that in 1846, however, "receiving the immersion of Pedobaptists and Campbellites" was with few exceptions "general throughout the South."[6] His strong opposition to this practice reversed the situation, according to his report. "I do not believe that there is one association *in the whole South* that would today indorse an alien immersion as scriptural or valid," he wrote in 1880.[7]

This matter is still very controversial, especially among Baptists in the South. Several associations in recent years have disfellowshiped churches for accepting "alien immersions," but most state conventions and the Southern Baptist Convention have refused to make it a matter of fellowship. It is not at all unusual for Baptist papers to print editorials regarding the practice, however. The editor of *The Baptist Messenger* (Oklahoma), for example, recently noted that most American, Conservative, GARB, English, and Canadian Baptist churches "accept any believer who has been immersed without further question regardless of who administered the baptism." While admitting that some Southern Baptist churches follow the same practice, he asserted that "this is not best for the individuals or the churches."[8]

Is baptism sacramental or symbolic? Baptists have historically defended a symbolic interpretation. "It is an act of obedience symbolizing the believer's faith in a crucified, buried, and risen Saviour, the believer's death to sin, the burial of the old life, and the resurrection to walk in newness of life in Christ Jesus," affirms the "Baptist Faith and Message."[9] Baptism does not confer or complete conversion but takes place after conversion. "Blood before water" is one way that this fact has been expressed. Only Thomas Helwys among Baptist leaders of the seventeenth century regarded baptism as essential to salvation. In repeated conflicts with followers of Alexander Campbell in the nineteenth century, Baptists reaffirmed their traditional viewpoint. More recently, English Baptist George R. Beasley-Murray has argued on the basis of New Testament evidence that "baptism and conversion are thus inseparables"[10] and that baptism is not "a purely symbolic rite." However he also admits that "such a judgment runs counter to the popular tradition of the Denomination to which the writer belongs."[11] Although some Baptists today question whether baptism is *merely* or *simply* a symbol, the fact remains that an essentially symbolic interpretation prevails.

Views of baptism have obvious implications for the Lord's Supper. *Should communion be open or closed, that is, should all Christians be allowed to participate or should the observance be confined to Baptists?* From the beginning, Baptist churches and leaders have disagreed on this matter. Seldom has it been made a matter of fellowship. Baptists who regard valid baptism as prerequisite to the Supper and insist that only believers' baptism by immersion is valid naturally confine the Supper in Baptist churches to Baptists only. William Kiffin, Abraham Booth, Joseph Ivimey, Joseph Kinghorn, and James B. Taylor are typical advocates of this point of view. In contrast, however, Henry Jessey, John Bunyan, Robert Hall, George Gould, and Charles Spurgeon are among those who have defended open communion. The prevailing practice in England until the mid-nineteenth century was closed communion, but since that time open communion has been most prevalent. In America, closed communion was virtually the universal practice until the twentieth century, but widespread diversity has been present for the past half-century.

J. R. Graves, about a century ago, advocated a more restricted view by limiting participation to members of the local Baptist church. Even Baptists were not allowed to partake of the Supper except in the churches where they were members. Although this position had limited influence, his insistence upon the Supper as a *church* ordinance prevailed to the extent that associations and conventions ceased observing the ordinance at their meetings. Although exceptions appear occasionally, most Baptists in America (especially in the South) refrain from participating in private, denominational, or ecumenical observances and consider the Supper as a part of the worship of a local congregation. Among Southern Baptists, closed communion theoretically predominates, but often the elements are distributed with no comments made or questions asked about terms of communion. Likewise, individual Baptists who attend services of worship in non-Baptist churches often participate in observing the Supper if invited or allowed to do so.

Is the Lord's Supper to be interpreted sacramentally or symbolically? Most Baptists would respond in favor of a symbolic interpretation, but many are seeking to underscore to a greater degree the significance of the Supper in the life of the believer and the worship of the church. Such efforts have raised questions about the meaning and/or form of the observance. Baptist writers in recent decades have insisted repeatedly that *mere* symbolism is not sufficient. This has led some to abandon what they regard as a "Zwinglian" view in favor of a "Calvinistic" or "spiritual" interpretation. Others have declared that Christ is really present in the Supper, though they have denied that any change takes place in the elements (transubstantiation) and have not been very clear about how Christ is present in any unique way. Baptists have retained a remarkable openness in interpreting the meaning of the Supper, and almost every view short of transubstantiation has been advocated.

Experimentation in form is another way that Baptist churches and leaders have sought to emphasize the significance of the Supper. Many churches today devote an entire service of worship to the observance, interspersing comments or Scripture readings at appropriate places. Occasionally a full meal is followed by an observance of the ordinance. Within recent years, I have participated in observances where the entire congregation sits around a table, where small groups gather at the front of the sanctuary and partake together, and where the elements are distributed to the entire congregation which remains seated (the more normal practice). At times one loaf and one cup are used; at other times crackers and grape juice are distributed. Most often an ordained minister leads in the service, though exceptions are not unusual. In form as well as meaning, diversity is evident.

Theological Problems

Individual Baptist writers have contributed frequently to discussions involving baptism and/or the Lord's Supper. Likewise, in several systematic theologies or in volumes dealing with ecclesiology, Baptist authors have included brief sections dealing with the ordinances. The fact remains, however, that no extensive work has been written by or for Baptists which interprets the biblical evidence, traces historical developments, identifies crucial issues, and provides a defensible theology for the theory and practice of Christian ordinances in Baptist churches.[12]

A unified theology is needed which makes clear what can be said about both ordinances and what can be said about each. Rather than dealing with subsidiary issues in a fragmented fashion, such a theology must focus attention upon the meaning of and authority for the ordinances. Christ instituted both ordinances, both portray publically and visibly the essential elements of the gospel, and both symbolize realities involving divine activity and human experience. Baptism is a once-for-all experience, but the Lord's Supper is repeated many times. Baptism follows closely one's profession of faith in Christ and actually in the New Testament was the declaration of that faith. The Lord's Supper declares one's continuing dependence upon the Christ proclaimed in the gospel, who died, was buried, and rose for our salvation.

Questions involving proper participants, acceptable administrators, permissible forms, and so forth must be answered in light of the meaning of the ordinances, which in turn should be based upon biblical theology rather than traditional practice. What determines the extent to which restoration to exact New Testament practices is determinative? Why should baptism be by immersion but not necessarily in the Jordan River? Why may crackers and grape juice be substituted for unleavened bread and wine? What church authorized Philip to baptize the eunuch into its membership? Who said that baptism must precede the Lord's Supper? Were administrators of baptism and the Lord's Supper *ordained* in the sense that this term indicates today? Should baptism be delayed to allow for a period of instruction following a profession of faith in Christ, thus departing from New Testament practice? Are modifications in baptismal practice valid for children reared in Christian homes? These are the kinds of questions that come to mind as needing fuller serious consideration by a people concerned about biblical teaching.

The significance of baptism and the Lord's Supper will not be increased simply by adopting sacramental language or shifting traditional forms. Significance will increase when Baptist churches and people commit themselves anew to the Christ proclaimed by the gospel and recognize that in observing the ordinances they are presenting in a unique way the gospel of Christ, committing themselves fully to its demands, and calling upon Christ the Savior and Lord to provide strength and leadership for the people of God individually and collectively for faithful service in his world.

Notes

1. See Karl Barth, *The Teaching of the Church Regarding Baptism* (London: SCM Press, 1948); Kurt Aland, *Did the Early Church Baptize Infants?* (London: SCM Press, 1963).
2. See Robert C. Walton, *The Gathered Community* (London: Carey Press, 1946); A. Gilmore, *Baptism and Christian Unity* (Valley Forge: The Judson Press, 1966).
3. Warren Carr, *Baptism: Conscience and Clue for the Church* (New York: Holt, Rinehart and Winston, 1964).
4. H. Wheeler Robinson, *Baptist Principles* (London: The Carey Kingsgate Press, 1938), p. 5.
5. *The Baptist Faith and Message* (Nashville: The Sunday School Board of the Southern Baptist Convention, 1963), p. 13.

6. J. R. Graves, *Old Landmarkism: What Is It?* (Texarkana: Baptist Sunday School Committee, 1880), p. xiv.

7. Ibid., p. xv.

8. "Baptists and Alien Immersion," *Baptist Messenger,* 6 October, 1977, p. 2.

9. *The Baptist Faith and Message,* p. 13.

10. G. R. Beasley-Murray, *Baptism in the New Testament* (Grand Rapids: William B. Eerdmans Publishing Company, 1973), p. 394.

11. Ibid., p. 263.

12. A partial exception is Neville Clark, *An Approach to the Theology of the Sacraments* (London: SCM Press Ltd., 1956). Books dealing with baptism are numerous, and a few deal with the Lord's Supper.

8

Southern Baptists and the Charismatic Movement

The charismatic movement continues to receive at least honorable mention in listings of top religious stories. An ecumenical Conference on Charismatic Renewal in the Christian Churches convened in Kansas City, Missouri, in July 1977 and reportedly attracted almost forty thousand charismatics, including perhaps eight hundred Baptists. Leaders estimate that among a constituency of some ten million charismatics in the United States, about half belong to classical Pentecostal groups and the remainder are evenly divided between Roman Catholics and mainline Protestants.[1] Results of a survey published in July 1977 by the Home Mission Board indicated that perhaps one hundred Southern Baptist churches with about ten thousand members are charismatic, though "closet" or secret charismatics might conceivably equal this number.[2]

The movement has been attracting the attention of the general public for about two decades. In the June 9, 1958, issue of *Life* magazine, Henry P. Van Dusen described a "third force" in Christendom ranging from emotional Pentecostals to sober Adventists. Noting the phenomenal growth of this diverse group, Van Dusen asserted that "they are one of the most important facts in the Christian history of our times."[3] In 1960, Dennis Bennett, an Episcopal rector in Van Nuys, California, resigned his position after professing an experience of Spirit baptism evidenced by speaking in tongues. Neo-Pentecostalism spread rapidly from that time among mainline Protestant groups and soon was making a profound impact upon Roman Catholics. An annual National Catholic Pentecostal Conference begun in 1967 was attended by more than thirty-five thousand charismatics in 1976. Catholic Pentecostals worship freely with Protestants in charismatic gatherings, and 46 percent of those attending the Kansas City conference referred to previously were Roman Catholics.

National and regional meetings, books and articles, prominent personalities, and powerful organizations are evidences of the vitality of the charismatic movement. Few geographical areas or religious groups have escaped the influence of the movement entirely. Southern Baptists are not among the exceptions. The thesis of this chapter, however, is that the movement has made a relatively slight impact upon Southern Baptist life and that this impact is declining.

Small groups of charismatics have emerged in many Southern Baptist congregations, often creating fear and frustration. In some cases, these groups have withdrawn to begin charismatic churches in adjacent areas. Where pastors have been among the charismatics, the churches in some instances have become charismatic; more often the pastors with some followers have formed other churches. Not a single Southern Baptist association or state convention to my knowledge is dominated by charismatics. No prominent Southern Baptist denominational leader has professed a Pentecostal experience and encouraged others to do so. Individual charismatics may be found in denominational agencies, but they are few in number and seldom propagate their views. Seminary professors, editors, and other denominational leaders have uniformly dissociated themselves from charismatics, even when they encourage understanding, fellowship, and cooperation.

The charismatic experience might be defined in such a way that every Christian is a charismatic. For analytical purposes, however, a definition along these lines is not very helpful. The focus of this chapter is upon those who regard the baptism of the Spirit as a second blessing beyond conversion and consider speaking in tongues (glossolalia) as the evidence of this blessing. Those who profess a second experience often emphasize other gifts such as healing, casting out demons, and prophecy.

Southern Baptists have been molded by the Reformed tradition modified by revivalism and evangelicalism. Historically, they have stressed a personal religious experience (born again) and the authority of Scripture, while actively promoting evangelism and missions. In many respects, a charismatic experience is foreign to Southern Baptist life, stressing a second blessing where Baptists prize the first. Charismatic experience tends to establish a spiritual elite by distinguishing between Christians who have had the experience and those who have not; Baptists stress the equality of all believers in Christ. The focus of the charismatic tends to be inward and upon believers; Southern Baptist concern is outward, directed toward the world. Baptists at times have been reductionist in theology and scriptural interpretation, but they are suspicious of an over-concentration upon the Holy Spirit in light of a few isolated texts. Charismatics often are critical of or indifferent to denominationalism while Southern Baptists are strongly attached to denominational structures and programs.

Testimonies from Baptists who have become charismatic indicate that often they had reached a point of dissatisfaction with their spiritual pilgrimage and were searching for something more.[4] At times a crisis experience, such as illness in the family, was involved. Contact with individual Pentecostals or an organization like Full Gospel Business Men's Fellowship International, the reading of literature written by charismatic Christians, or listening to prominent personalities like Pat Boone or David Wilkerson or Oral Roberts by means of television or radio encouraged them to seek the baptism of the Spirit. Usually they were assisted in reaching a climactic experience accompanied by ecstatic utterances with the encouragement of those who already professed such an experience. In other words, the experience came as a result of unhappiness within Southern Baptist life combined with encounters outside rather than as a natural development of a vital and growing spiritual life undergirded by Bible study, Christian fellowship, and personal devotion. However, I would not account for the popularity of the charismatic movement only in terms of widespread failure of the churches to meet the spiritual and emotional needs of their people.

To say that the impact of charismatics upon Southern Baptist life has been slight is not to argue that the movement has not created widespread interest and concern. The charismatic claims for biblical justification would be sufficient to attract Baptists' attention to what the Bible actually teaches in this area. Seminary professors faced these claims at an early stage, as students influenced by charismatic groups on college campuses arrived at the seminaries. At times tension was evident within student bodies and between students and faculty members. Professors responded by addressing the issue in chapel services, offering special classes, writing books and articles, and counseling with students.

Following discussions in the Faculty Club, three professors at The Southern Baptist Theological Seminary published a book entitled *Glossolalia* in 1967, which examined speaking in tongues from biblical, historical, and psychological perspectives.[5] Described as "an objective but understanding treatment of the subject in a nonpartisan way,"[6] the book provides little consolation for contemporary charismatics. Frank Stagg distinguished tongues at Pentecost and in Corinth, describing the first as intelligible language utilized in preaching the gospel and the second as unintelligible, ecstatic utterance. "The shame of Corinth is not to be cloaked with the glory of Pentecost. Babbling, ancient or modern, is Corinthian and not Pentecostal."[7] The Holy Spirit is available to all and should produce the fruits of the Spirit (Gal. 5). Speaking in tongues is recognized as a spiritual gift but as the least gift, not to be sought. Glenn Hinson identified outbreaks of glossolalia at infrequent intervals in Christian history. "If it is indeed to be seen as an evidence of the Holy Spirit's work," he inquired, "why did it have such an inconsistent and intermittent history?"[8] The gift has not aided the church in accomplishing its mission. Those who speak in tongues should do so for their own edification, taking care not to offend others. Wayne Oates interpreted glossolalia as resulting from religious repression and compared it to childlike language. He suggested "a thoroughgoing reaffirmation of the total doctrine of the Holy Spirit and its function in the life of the church" as the best antidote.[9]

Dale Moody published *Spirit of the Living God* the next year (1968, republished 1976), primarily interpreting biblical materials but with an awareness of the charismatic revival in progress. "I have tried to avoid extremes in both directions at this point," he stated, "but I'm sure my sympathies are more with those who long for renewal and a deeper awareness of the living God in daily life. Careful scholarship and the charismatic community can be united, and this is a great need of our time."[10] Moody argues that tongues in Acts and 1 Corinthians are the same and that they are not foreign languages but ecstatic utterances understandable through the gift of interpretation. A nonrepeatable baptism of the Spirit is distinguished from frequent or continuous filling of the Spirit. "Paul seeks to regulate tongues, not to eliminate them," he said. "Modern crusaders who seek to drive from the church all who receive the gift of tongues . . . confront difficulties with Paul."[11]

But a word of caution is also stated in the other direction. "Pentecostals who major on the examples in Acts and minimize the evaluations and regulations of 1 Corinthians, chapter 14, bring upon themselves many of their calamities."[12] Moody is obviously sympathetic with the current emphasis upon the place of the Holy Spirit in the life of the church and regards gifts of speaking in tongues and healing as valid. On the other hand, he does not appear to regard such a gift as a second blessing or as evidence that one has been baptized in the Spirit.

Stagg addressed the issue again in a broader context in 1973 by publishing *The Holy Spirit Today*. Interpreting baptism in and filled with the Spirit as interchangeable concepts in the New Testament, he argued that such an experience is not restricted to a few, is not a second blessing, and does not produce sinlessness or lead to unintelligible tongues. Every Christian is charismatic for "charismatic gifts are the gifts of God to us."[13] He not only defends the right of one to advocate speaking in tongues but also the right of another to warn against dangers in such a practice. "Speaking in tongues is the privilege and responsibility of those who choose them," he asserted, "but this writer cannot conscientiously commend modern glossolalia."[14]

Fisher Humphreys and Malcolm Tolbert published the book *Speaking in Tongues* after teaching a special course at New Orleans Seminary related to this matter in January 1973. The book was designed as a practical aid for pastors and laymen to assist them in understanding Pentecostals and biblical teachings about speaking in tongues. The authors desired to be "fair and understanding" and to "contribute something to Christian fellowship."[15] After defining speaking in tongues, they dealt with some thirty biblical and practical questions related to the phenomenon.

Noting that Jesus did not mention glossolalia, that Acts 2 is not applicable to the contemporary practice, and that serious limitations were imposed by Paul for the practice at Corinth, the authors questioned or challenged virtually every major proposition accepted by modern Pentecostals. Although asserting that a church should have room for diversity in belief and practice, they stressed its responsibility to prevent divisions, initiate preventive programs, and protect itself from campaigns designed to promote tongues-speaking in the congregation.

God's Spirit in You published in 1975 by Landrum Leavell is a series of sermons based on selected New Testament passages related to the ministry of the Holy Spirit. "Since Jesus said the Holy Spirit would not speak of himself but would glorify Christ," he stated, "I believe any teaching that exalts the Holy Spirit above Jesus Christ is a tragic departure from the New Testament."[16] Every Christian has been baptized of the Spirit, but glossolalia is not for everyone. The possibility of sinlessness is denied, and sanctification is not to be considered as a second work of grace.

Responses to four articles on the Holy Spirit, in light of the charismatic movement, written by Terry Young in 1975 encouraged him to publish *The Spirit Within You* two years later. "It is the position of this book that there ought to be a vitality in the Christian life as an outgrowth of the experience of salvation," he asserted. "This vitality is inherent in the experience of salvation itself. It does not await some later experience, or second blessing, to bring about the intimacy of walking with God in a warm, vital relationship."[17]

Young discusses the Holy Spirit from biblical and theological perspectives with a sensitivity to current discussions and problems. "One reason for the appeal of the charismatic movement is that there is a fertile field among church members whose level of maturity is woefully retarded."[18] Pentecost cannot be repeated. Paul recognized the validity of the gift of tongues at Corinth but considered it a minor gift which did not edify but divided the church. The practice of tongues is immature, childish, not a mark of spiritual maturity. It should be practiced only under stringent regulations.

As to the contemporary practice, "in most cases those who have spoken in tongues received the gift after eagerly and earnestly seeking it. They were psychologically conditioned to speak in tongues," which is a "spiritual crutch."[19] Christians have received the Spirit at conversion and should allow him to control their lives, accepting the power provided to produce the fruits of the Spirit.

John Newport wrote a perceptive article for *Home Missions* in May, 1965, regarding speaking in tongues. Major presuppositions of contemporary charismatics were challenged in this article also. Pentecost represents a special miracle for a special occasion, and 1 Corinthians 12—14 should be the primary document for understanding other manifestations of speaking in tongues. "As evangelicals we cannot deny the biblical record regarding tongues, nor are we disposed to do so," he said. "It is one thing to acknowledge that fact, however, and quite another to accept the contemporary pentecostal displays as valid expressions of the New Testament spiritual gifts."[20] A later article (1971) accounted for interest in glossolalia in sociological factors associated with rapid change, desire for other means of expression as the authority of words decline, and reactions to nonparticipation in culture and church life. Newport's evaluation of glossolalia used terms, such as escapism, childishness, and self-righteousness. Positively, the phenomenon should teach Christians the importance of understanding, accepting, and loving all kinds of people; of participating actively in constructive Christian work; and of maintaining a future-oriented world view.[21]

A sermon preached by J. W. MacGorman in chapel at Southwestern Baptist Theological Seminary in 1971 was expanded into the book, *The Gifts of the Spirit* (1974). MacGorman is not a glossolalist but proposes an irenic approach. Glossolalia is regarded as one gift among many. God determines who receives what gifts. Those who have not experienced glossolalia should not quench the Spirit. Those who have should not distort the Spirit. A strong plea is made that glossolalia not be made a test of fellowship by either party. "It will be uncomfortable for us as Baptists if we exclude people from our associations and churches for claiming a New Testament experience."[22]

Seminary professors have contributed to other publications which can only be mentioned in passing. *Tongues,* edited by Luther Dyer in 1971, contains not only a chapter by Newport previously mentioned but others by Wayne Ward, Hugh Wamble, and Morris Ashcraft. Wamble interprets neo-Pentecostalism as "one outgrowth of restive Christians search for spiritual dimension which they had not found in their churches, but which they had been taught to expect."[23] Glossolalia is "a by-product of Pentecostalism" and belongs "on historic Christianity's outer fringe."[24] Ward presents various views of tongue speaking, and Ashcraft interprets the biblical materials in Acts and Corinthians.

Doctoral dissertations written at various seminaries have also resulted in additional publications. An article by Fred Meeks in the recent issue of the *Southwestern Journal*, "The Pastor and the Tongues Movement," is one such example.[25] Another is several articles and two helpful books by Watson E. Mills of Averett College: *Understanding Speaking in Tongues* (1972) and *Speaking in Tongues: Let's Talk About It* (1973).[26] *Testing Tongues by the Word* by Jimmy A. Millikan also began in this way.[27]

Seminary professors have not been alone in addressing issues created by the charismatic movement. Recent presidents of the Southern Baptist Convention have invariably been questioned concerning their attitude toward charismatics. Jaroy Weber (1975, 1976) was quoted widely as stating that "charismatics should get right or get out."[28] Indicating that he was misquoted, Weber expressed his conviction that "within our structure there is enough elasticity for people who differ in some of the teachings of the word of God."[29] He welcomed renewed interest in the Holy Spirit but asserted the right of majorities, as well as minorities, to interpret biblical materials and personal experiences related to the Spirit.

We need to instruct our people on the meaning of baptism and the filling of the Spirit. When a person is converted, he is baptized into the body of Christ, baptized of the Holy Spirit.... As we develop we have filling experiences as often as we surrender. It is not a matter of praying God's Spirit down but a willingness to become aware of his evident presence and a willingness to let Him control our lives.[30]

While Weber sought to be conciliatory, former president W. A. Criswell (1969, 1970) castigated the charismatic experience of speaking in tongues as "senseless, inane and idiotic."[31] "They think I am naive. They think they can fool me into thinking that gibberish is a language," he declared. "If that is the Christian faith, then I am not a Christian. Exclamation point."[32] The charismatic movement was branded as "near heresy" by the outspoken Dallas pastor. When questioned about his evaluation of this statement, Weber confessed, "I feel he spoke the sentiments of about 95 percent of the pastors in the Southern Baptist Convention, including me."[33] Weber abhorred divisive, disruptive aspects of the movement and felt that the response called for was proper biblical teaching and leadership at the local church level rather than the adoption of resolutions by associations or conventions.

In a series of articles entitled "Baptists Beliefs," published in state papers, Herschel Hobbs communicated his views "concerning spirituals" by interpreting 1 Corinthians 12—15. In these articles, Hobbs argued that tongues at Pentecost and in Corinth were the same, in each case involving language spoken on earth rather than heavenly language known only to God.

"However one may regard tongues at Corinth," he said, "there is no similarity between this gift and 'modern' tongues." The gift of tongues was regarded by Paul as the lowest gift of all and is of practically no value to the church today. "If the ability to speak in a foreign language without having studied it were given today, why not to foreign missionaries?"[34]

Issues other than the charismatic movement have been paramount among Southern Baptists under presidents James L. Sullivan (1977) and Jimmy Allen (1978, 1979). Allen indicated, following his election in 1977, that he was not at all threatened by the movement. "There's been a real fresh moving of the Holy Spirit in a great many places within our fellowship for which I'm very grateful," he said. "There are some bizarre behavior patterns which create all sorts of controversy," he continued. "When that happens, I want to ask what the highest good is—what's happening in the total witness of their lives."[35]

Pastors and other denominational leaders have not been reticent in describing what should happen or what does happen with a renewed emphasis on the ministry of the Holy Spirit. Books published by Broadman Press other than those already mentioned include *The Spirit-Filled Trauma* by Robert L. Hamblin with a foreward by Carl Bates; *Understanding Tongues-Speaking* by C. W. Parnell; *This Gift Is Mine* by Ralph W. Neighbour, Jr.; *After the Spirit Comes* by Jack R. Taylor; *No Second-Class Christians* by Lynn A. Clayton; and *A Search for Common Ground* by M. Thomas Starkes. These books are positive in their stress upon the ministry of the Spirit, but their evaluation of the contemporary charismatic movement differs little from other works already analyzed.[36]

The charismatic movement appears to have peaked among Southern Baptists in 1975-1976, following a series of strong actions by several associations. At least five associations in four states excluded charismatic churches from their membership. Three other associations adopted statements of disapproval or warning. At annual meetings in 1974, the Dallas Baptist Association branded the movement as disruptive and the Rogers Association in northeast Oklahoma labeled it heresy.[37] Charismatic churches were requested to withdraw voluntarily from association membership. When this did not take place, the Dallas Association, in October 1975, proceeded to disfellowship the Beverly Hills and Shady Grove churches.[38] The Cincinnati Association in Ohio also withdrew fellowship from two churches, Oak Hills and Saylor Park.[39] In Louisiana, the Trenton Association in West Monroe ousted the Claiborne Church, and the Plaquemines Association excluded Empire.[40] College Heights Baptist Church in Ventura, California, was also excluded by the Harmony Association. The Union Association of Houston, Texas, condemned the movement as "of the devil," and the Guadalupe Association warned churches against involvement in charismatic practices.[41]

In most cases, state conventions have refrained from adopting resolutions addressed directly to the charismatic movement. Maryland Baptists rejected charismatic involvement as a test of fellowship, while the Arizona Convention "encouraged Southern Baptist pastors to preach and teach the doctrine of the Holy Spirit to counter 'disunity' sometimes caused by 'pseudo-charismatic' movements."[42] Messengers to the Texas Baptist Convention in 1976 overruled a recommendation by its credentials committee to seat representatives from two charismatic churches ousted by the Dallas Association.[43] Most state conventions, however, as well as the Southern Baptist Convention, have appeared content to allow local churches and associations to deal with problems as they arise. Most of the charismatic churches disfellowshiped by associations consider themselves as still belonging to the respective state conventions and the Southern Baptist Convention.

Faced by increasing opposition, charismatic churches and pastors encouraged one another by convening a series of regional and national conferences. Two regional meetings were hosted by Pastor Ray Lambeth and Trinity Baptist Church of Fern Creek in Louisville, Kentucky, in November 1974 and February 1975. An attendance of about 500 was reported at the first and over 800 at the second.[44] A third meeting at the Claiborne Church, West Monroe, Louisiana, was in progress with about 850 persons present when the Trenton Association excluded the church.[45] These churches were joined by the Beverly Hills Church of Dallas, Texas; Bay View Heights Church, Mobile, Alabama; and West Lauderdale Church, Fort Lauderdale, Florida, in sponsoring the first National Southern Baptist Charismatic Conference. The conference was held in Dallas, Texas, July 21-24, 1976, and reportedly attracted over 2000 participants from at least 15 states.[46] A second such conference in 1977, also in Dallas, involved about 3,500 delegates from 37 states and 4 other countries, according to its leaders.[47] Such gatherings will undoubtedly continue, but whether the churches and pastors involved will eventually withdraw from the Southern Baptist Convention is not clear at this point. At present they regard themselves as loyal Southern Baptists who have not deviated from the doctrinal consensus expressed in the "Baptist Faith and Message" approved by the Convention in 1963.

Southern Baptists are a diverse fellowship, and this diversity is reflected in their appraisal of the charismatic movement. A general consensus based upon what they have said and done, however, appears to include the following elements. First, they react positively toward a renewed emphasis upon the Holy Spirit and agree that in the past they have given too little attention to the work of the Spirit in the life of believers and churches. Second, they affirm anew that a believer is baptized of the Spirit in conversion and requires no second blessing subsequent to that experience. Third, many of them would agree that repeated fillings of the Spirit are possible, but such experiences are largely equated with deeper consecration, commitment, or commissioning for special tasks, resulting in a greater awareness of God's presence and leadership.

Fourth, they would not deny that speaking in tongues is a biblical gift, but they note that it is a very minor gift that should be restricted in use, not actively sought, and not claimed as an evidence of the baptism of the Spirit. It is not a uniquely Christian gift since it is often practiced in other religions. Fifth, most affirm that tongues in Acts and 1 Corinthians are different, the former being understandable language and the latter ecstatic utterance. Modern tongues are regarded as Corinthian, that is, not actual language. Some interpreters argue that tongues in Acts and 1 Corinthians are the same and are actual languages, while others assert that both were ecstatic utterances.

Six, none deny the power of God to heal but most are skeptical about claims of healing gifts and special services where individuals are declared healed. Seven, most regard the charismatic movement as divisive, encouraging spiritual pride and stressing a minor gift out of proportion to the biblical evidence. Eight, charismatics are to be tolerated and loved as Christian brothers but not be allowed to disrupt fellowship and engage in militant proselytizing activities. Finally, local Baptist pastors and churches have the primary responsibility for dealing with problems that arise in connection with the movement, and a preventative approach emphasizing biblical exegesis and Christian nurture while engaging in meaningful worship and witness will enable believers to identify and utilize gifts of God's grace in a manner that will honor Christ and edify the church.

Notes

1. *The Christian Century,* 17-24 August 1977, p. 707.
2. Tim Nicholas, "Singing in the Spirit," *Home Missions* (July-August 1976): 36.
3. *Life,* 9 June 1958, p. 122.
4. See, for example, *The Acts of the Holy Spirit Among the Baptists Today* (Los Angeles: Full Gospel Business Men's Fellowship International, 1971).
5. Frank Stagg, E. Glenn Hinson, and Wayne E. Oates, *Glossolalia: Tongue-Speaking in Biblical, Historical, and Psychological Perspective* (Nashville: Abingdon Press, 1967).
6. Ibid., p. 9.
7. Ibid., p. 41.
8. Ibid., p. 74.
9. Ibid., p. 99.

10. Dale Moody, *Spirit of the Living God: What the Bible Says About the Spirit* (Nashville: Broadman Press, 1976), p. 10.
11. Ibid., pp. 100-101.
12. Ibid., p. 101.
13. Frank Stagg, *The Holy Spirit Today* (Nashville: Broadman Press, 1973), p. 24.
14. Ibid., p. 55.
15. Fisher Humphreys and Malcolm Tolbert, *Speaking in Tongues* (Zachary, Louisiana: Christian Litho, Inc., 1973), p. vii.
16. Landrum P. Leavell, *God's Spirit in You* (Nashville: Broadman Press, 1974), p. vii.
17. J. Terry Young, *The Spirit Within You* (Nashville: Broadman Press, 1977), p. 6.
18. Ibid., p. 51.
19. Ibid., pp. 97,98.
20. John P. Newport, "Speaking with Tongues," *Home Missions* 36 (May 1965): 22.
21. Luther B. Dyer, editor, *Tongues* (Jefferson City, Missouri: LeRoy Publishers, 1971), pp. 105-127.
22. Jack W. MacGorman, *The Gifts of the Spirit* (Nashville: Broadman Press, 1974), p. 6.
23. Dyer, p. 47.
24. Ibid., pp. 47,53.
25. Fred E. Meeks, "The Pastor and the Tongues Movement" *Southwestern Journal of Theology* (Spring, 1977), pp. 73-85.
26. Watson E. Mills, *Understanding Speaking in Tongues* (Grand Rapids: William B. Eerdmans Publishing Co., 1972) and *Speaking in Tongues: Let's Talk About It* (Waco: Word Books, 1973).
27. Jimmie A. Millikan, *Testing Tongues by the Word* (Nashville: Broadman Press, 1973).
28. *Baptist Standard,* 1 January 1975, p. 11.
29. Ibid.
30. Ibid.
31. *Baptist Standard,* 23 April 1974.
32. Ibid.
33. *Baptist Standard,* 18 June 1975, p. 7.
34. *Baptist Standard,* 18 February 1976.
35. *Biblical Recorder,* 25 June 1977, p. 5.
36. See Robert L. Hamblin, *The Spirit-Filled Trauma* (Nashville: Broadman Press, 1974); C. W. Parnell, *Understanding Tongues-Speaking* (Nashville: Broadman Press, n.d.); Ralph W. Neighbour, Jr., *This Gift Is Mine* (Nashville: Broadman Press, 1974); Jack R. Taylor, *After the Spirit Comes*

(Nashville: Broadman Press, 1974); and M. Thomas Starkes, *A Search for Common Ground* (Nashville: Broadman Press, 1977); and Lynn P. Clayton, *No Second-Class Christians* (Nashville: Broadman Press, 1976).

37. *Biblical Recorder,* 9 November 1974, p. 8.
38. *Baptist Standard,* 29 December 1975, p. 4.
39. Ibid.
40. *Baptist Standard,* 21 July 1976, p. 4.
41. See *Baptist Standard,* 29 November 1975, p. 4, and 12 November 1975, p. 5.
42. Nicholas, p. 44.
43. *Alabama Baptist,* 28 October 1976.
44. *Baptist Press,* 3 November 1975.
45. Ibid.
46. *Alabama Baptist,* 5 August 1976.
47. *The Baptist World,* November 1977, p. 11.

9

Critical Issues in Southern Baptist Life

The Southern Baptist Convention was formed in 1845 in Augusta, Georgia. Approximately 350,000 members in slightly over 4100 churches were scattered throughout 15 states at that time. Mission boards established at Richmond, Virginia, and Marion, Alabama, reported to the Convention but largely raised their own funds and administered their affairs between triennial meetings of the Convention. These meetings became biennial in 1849 and annual from 1866. A Bible Board was established at Nashville, Tennessee, in 1851 which survived until 1863. In the latter year a Sunday School Board began operation at Greenville, South Carolina, but was abolished after a decade.

Agencies formed outside the Convention structure during the nineteenth century included the Southern Baptist Publication Society (1847) located at Charleston, South Carolina; the Southern Baptist Sunday School Union (1851) at Nashville, Tennessee; and The Southern Baptist Theological Seminary (1859) at Greenville, South Carolina. The latter institution moved to Louisville, Kentucky, in 1877 and was eventually incorporated into the Convention (1927). The Woman's Missionary Union, not entirely by choice, was formed auxiliary to the Convention (1888) and has so remained.

Two additional boards have been established. The Sunday School Board began in 1891 at Nashville, Tennessee, and the Annuity Board, located in Dallas, Texas, dates from 1918. The Home Mission Board was moved to Atlanta, Georgia, in 1880. Other agencies (institutions, commissions, committees) have been formed as needs arose so that the Convention presently works through nineteen agencies. Directors or trustees elected by the Convention are responsible for administering the

affairs of the various agencies, who report annually to the Convention.
Southern Baptist membership currently exceeds 13 million in over
35,000 churches, almost 1200 associations, and 34 state conventions.
Supported through the Cooperative Program (from 1925) and assisted
by the Executive Committee (from 1917), this complex organizational
structure functions with substantial efficiency and freedom. Measured by
widely accepted standards, the Southern Baptist Convention has been
eminently successful and highly productive as a Christian denomination.

Southern Baptists have not been without problems, however, at any
point in their history. The issue of slavery, with all its ramifications, resulted in the Convention being formed. Landmarkism created dissen-
tion for a half century and is not without influence even today. War and
reconstruction threatened the very existence of the Convention for
several decades. Southern Baptist expansion in the United States and
the refusal to participate in ecumenical organizations produced tension
with other Christian groups. Fundamentalists attacked liberals and social
conservatives resisted the Social Gospel. World conflict and cold war,
depression and inflation, secularism and sectarianism have provided a
continuing agenda for discussion and response.

The fact that Southern Baptists have faced critical issues in the past
should provide perspective for understanding those of the present but
should not undermine the seriousness of comtemporary concerns. A
variety of issues is important to segments of the Convention constituency but several are critical enough to dominate, dissipate, or divide
Southern Baptists' resources. These may be stated as (1) Christ or culture—the Southern issue; (2) rights or responsibilities—the Baptist issue;
and (3) missions or orthodoxy—the Convention issue.

Christ or Culture—The Southern Issue

The classic analysis in *Christ and Culture* by H. Richard Niebuhr
identifies alternatives or possible relationships between the Christian
faith and culture.[1] Opposition and accommodation, respectively, are
categorized as "Christ against Culture" and "the Christ of Culture."
Synthesis and paradox are characterized as "Christ above Culture" and
"Christ and Culture in Paradox." "Christ the Transformer of Culture"

presents the conversionist solution. Niebuhr recognized that these five types were, in the final analysis, artificial constructs to which no individual or group conforms totally. They do identify, however, "the continuity and significance of the great *motifs* that appear and reappear in the long wrestling of Christians with their enduring problem."[2]

Baptist responses to culture range from radical sectarianism (opposition) to an establishment mentality (accommodation), at various times reflecting tendencies toward synthesis, paradox, or transformation. The present focus upon Christ and culture as an issue in Southern Baptist life, however, is not intended as a sophisticated sociological analysis but as an attempt to explore some practical problems faced by Southern Baptists living in a changing cultural environment.

For one thing, while the Convention has expanded geographically, the dominant word in current images of Southern Baptists remains *Southern*. Cooperating churches exist in all fifty states, but about 90 percent of the churches and members are located in sixteen states. "Pioneer" areas include such states as New York, Pennsylvania, Illinois, and California. Churches outside the South appeal primarily to dislocated Southerners. Ministers are hesitant about accepting places of service in areas isolated from the southern locale. Attempts to change even the name of the Convention have failed repeatedly. The election of Jimmy Carter as president of the United States brought national notoriety to Southern Baptists, and the president himself, after conferring with denominational leaders, challenged the Convention in session at Kansas City, Missouri, (1977) to provide and fund five thousand additional mission volunteers by 1982. But whether the Convention will move toward a national rather than sectional orientation is not clear at this time.

Again, not only have Southern Baptists expanded outside the South but also Southern culture has been changing radically in the last three decades. A predominately rural, agrarian society is being replaced by an industrialized, urbanized one. The pattern of white supremacy accompanied by racial segregation has been altered substantially toward racial equality and social interchange. A religiously oriented culture has been challenged by religious pluralism and secularism. The solid South is no longer solid. By far the largest religious group in this locality, Southern

Baptists have not adapted easily to these rapidly changing conditions. Interpreters outside and inside the Southern Baptist Convention have tended to stereotype or caricature the denomination, regarding southernness not only as geographical but also as cultural. Southern Baptists have been described repeatedly for several decades as racists, individualists, fundamentalists, more interested in preserving the Southern way of life than in addressing crucial social problems. A typical statement by John Boles could be multiplied many times:

> The Southern Baptist Convention is today the nation's largest Protestant denomination and also the one most indigenous to the South. Today this church, like its sister evangelical denominations, is facing a crisis. Its ministers for the most part persist in preaching a literalism so strict it suffocates biblical relevancy. Their emphasis is almost wholly individualistic, patently ignoring social ills and injustices. Modern scientific and intellectual currents are often shunned, and the faithful are held to a pietism which obeys the letter of the Scriptures and misses the broader implications. The proudly autonomous local congregations calmly ignore the modernist social pronouncements which they know denominational leaders cannot enforce.[3]

An alleged absence of social concern is often set in contrast to an avid evangelistic emphasis, as though evangelism and social concern were mutually exclusive. A comment by Langdon Gilkey in 1963 and repeated by Samuel Hill a decade later illustrates this point.

> Some groups, notable in our day the Southern Baptists, have made evangelism the central core of the church, and their experience reveals the problem involved. For then ministers tend to be taught, not how to care for their flock by preaching, counseling, and worship, but how to evangelize—i.e., how to persuade other people to join the flock. And when these new members ask, "Now that I have joined, what am I to do?" the answer is apt to be "Go out among your neighbors and bring in some more"—who, presumably, will in turn themselves merely seek new additions among their neighbors. Being a Christian thus becomes merely the operation of expanding itself. And with this the religious reality of Christianity, both as a personal relation to God through the hearing of His Word and the worship of His glory, and the incarnating of that Word in acts of love and reconciliation, is in danger of being lost.[4]

Titles of the two best known analyses of Southern Baptist involvement in social concerns reflect stances of indifference and bondage. *At Ease in Zion* by Rufus Spain (1961) focused on the period from 1865 to 1900. Spain concluded that in this period Southern Baptists were

defenders of the status quo, whose political, social, and economic attitudes coincided with rather than challenged prevailing attitudes of
Southern society. "Their significance in Southern life consisted not in
their power to mold their environment to conform to their standards,"
he stated.[5] "Rather their importance as a social force was in supporting
and perpetuating the standards prevailing in society at large. Only on
matters involving personal conduct or narrow religious principles did
Baptists diverge noticeable from prevailing Southern views."[6]

John Lee Eighmy examined social attitudes from the origin of the
Convention to 1970 in *Churches in Cultural Captivity* (1972). An epi-
logue written by Samuel Hill describes the major thesis of the book as
"that Southern Baptist churches tend to reflect the values held by their
surrounding culture rather than to prompt critical assessment of those
values."[7] Eighmy himself advanced a somewhat more balanced view,
noting that Southern Baptists "have responded to social issues more
significantly than is generally recognized."[8] He indicated, however, that
pragmatic considerations in terms of polity and programs often rule out
involvement in controversial social issues that might undermine a broad
base of support in the churches.[9]

A perceptive article by Foy Valentine, executive director of the Christian Life Commission of the Southern Baptist Convention, recently
explored the latter point by examining the relation of Baptist polity and
social pronouncements.[10] Valentine agreed with Spain and Eighmy that
declarations on public issues by Southern Baptists correspond more
closely to sentiments of ordinary Baptists than do similar pronouncements by authoritarian bodies who formulate social positions on behalf
of their constituencies. After studying a multiplicity of resolutions,
recommendations, sermons, and statements, Valentine observed that
"Southern Baptists have been amazingly outspoken about social
issues."[11] "More than any other Baptist people in history, they have
developed an indigenous strength capable of supporting the development of self-awareness and self-confidence bordering on an established
church mind-set," he continued. "Therefore, there has been a willingness to move in on the culture at will, speak to it, rebuke it, shape it, correct it, support it, affirm it, and even keep it."[12]

No one knows better than Valentine the resistance that Southern

Baptists can generate when proposals differ substantially from popular sentiment. He is also keenly aware that a vast gulf exists between adopting pronouncements and translating them into action. But the fact is that progressive proposals continue to be made by individuals and groups with such intensity and regularity that they often merge with other forces to bring about change in the direction desired.

Southern Baptist social pronouncements never carry with them the authority and assurance of enforcement that some denominations, particularly authoritarian ones, carry with theirs. The only hope for implementation of Southern Baptist social pronouncements is the hope that they will convey moral authority, that they will be heard sympathetically and received willingly by Baptist people, that they will be perceived as the word of the Lord regarding a particular issue at a particular time. The pronouncements, primarily, have been educational tools in the hands of God-ordained and Baptist-ordained prophet-quarterbacks who originate them, shepherd them to some sort of public expression, and then utilize them to move Baptists, and sometimes the public at large, to desired attitudes and actions.[13]

As already indicated, the purpose of focusing upon the Southern issue is not to challenge or correct past interpretations or to commend or condemn Southern Baptists. It is, however, to stress the fact that a regional orientation and image from the past still persists while the region itself is being radically transformed and the denomination is becoming national. The following summary comments, therefore, are designed to provide reflections for understanding the past and proposals for facing the future.

First, Southern Baptists often have reflected cultural values, especially in matters of race relations. Too frequently they have followed rather than challenging social trends or proposing alternate ones. The fact that they have been accompanied in this by most Christian bodies should be a matter of regret and not comfort. Second, they are strongly committed to evangelism and hopefully will remain so, believing that vital change begins in lives as individuals trust Christ as Savior and Lord. But, this commitment should heighten rather than eliminate concern for the total person and the total society. Third, Baptist polity has insured that pronouncements and programs reflect more nearly sentiments of ordinary Baptists, which has tempered radical proposals and strengthened social conservatism.

Fourth, Southern Baptists throughout their history have expressed social concern and initiated social programs and activities. More often these have been on a selective basis, dealing more with personal morality than social structures, but a vast variety of problems and issues has been addressed. Fifth, Southern Baptists still have a long way to go in developing a social sensitivity and responding to social problems and needs at various levels, but they are probably more aware of opportunities and responsibilities in these areas today than at any time in their history. Any criticism to the effect that their responses deal more with results than causes may be admitted but should not undercut the significance of a variety of ministries offered and supported in the name of Christ.

Finally, Southern Baptists at the present time are faced with an unusual opportunity to contribute in communicating, interpreting, and applying the gospel to the nation and the world. This gospel, of course, must be the gospel of Christ, not simply the gospel of the Southern or even American culture.

Rights or Responsibilities—The Baptist Issue

British historian W. T. Whitley regarded the doctrine of the church as the distinctive feature of Baptists.[14] H. Wheeler Robinson, however, argued that their most distinguishing principle was believers' baptism by immersion.[15] Henry Cook did not deny the significance of either of these but stressed that behind them was an emphasis on the supremacy of the New Testament in all matters of faith and practice which constitutes the basis of the Baptist position.[16] For E. Y. Mullins the distinctive Baptist contribution was the principle of the competency of the soul in religion under God,[17] while others have suggested that the concept of religious freedom or of the lordship of Christ is of supreme significance.

Interpreters will probably never agree upon a single principle or statement as determinative; a particular emphasis or practice will be stressed according to current needs, interests, or problems. In such efforts, the Baptist heritage is usually scrutinized for support and, at least on a selective basis, historical precedent often is found. Thus the heritage is dynamic and living rather than static or dead. Danger arises, however, if some segment of Baptist life or thought is exaggerated to such an extent that other segments become blurred or lost.

In most cases, interpreters have proceeded from one basic principle or concept and deduced other beliefs or practices that Baptists advocate. E. Y. Mullins, for example, set forth six axioms of religion based on soul competency:

1. The theological axiom: The holy and loving God has a right to be sovereign.
2. The religious axiom: All souls have an equal right to direct access to God.
3. The ecclesiastical axiom: All believers have a right to equal privileges in the church.
4. The moral axiom: To be responsible man must be free.
5. The religio-civic axiom: A free Church in a free State.
6. The social axiom: Love your neighbor as yourself.[18]

Faced with a time of theological transition, ecclesiastical uncertainty, social adjustment, and religious diversity, Mullins emphasized rights under God of the individual, local church, and denomination. The individual was competent, the church autonomous, and denominational relationships totally voluntary. These ideas were congenial to Americans in general and to Baptists in particular. "To the extent that Baptists were to develop an apologetic for their church life during the early decades of the twentieth century, it was to be on the basis of this highly individualistic principle," the competency of the soul in religion under God.[19]

For Southern Baptists this approach has been viable and meaningful. Religion is interpreted in personal terms first and foremost as a relation between the individual and God, and every person has direct access to God in Jesus Christ. Each congregation is regarded as not simply a part of the church but the church in fact and in full, possessing authority under the lordship of Christ to constitute itself, determine membership, select officers, and order its affairs. Churches are not bound together in or through a sacerdotal or sacramental system but cooperate voluntarily through associations, state conventions, the Southern Baptist Convention, and Baptist World Alliance without any one entity infringing on the rights of another.

While this understanding sets forth and adequately protects significant rights of Baptists, equally important responsibilities may be obscured, ignored, or at least not emphasized. Herschel Hobbs must have sensed this fact in his recent revision of *The Axioms of Religion*. "The competency of the soul in religion entails the responsibility of the soul in religion," he observed.[20]

Since God is sovereign, he has the right to command his people. The equal right of all men to direct access to God means that we should make known that right to all men and defend it against any interference. Equal privilege in the church makes every believer equally responsible for what his church is doing in carrying out the Great Commission. Free believers are under obligation to obey God when he commands. A free church in a free state forbids churches to expect governments to do their God-given work for them. And we cannot love our neighbor as ourselves if we ignore his physical and spiritual needs.[21]

The call to Christian responsibility should be taken seriously by Southern Baptists at every level of denominational life and may be acknowledged and accepted without relinquishing essential rights. Individualism, autonomy, and voluntarism are to be interpreted from a biblical perspective that is appropriate for the people of God under the lordship of Jesus Christ and leadership of the Holy Spirit.

Winthrop Hudson, a prominent American Baptist historian and churchman, regards an approach based on soul competency as detrimental if not destructive. "The practical effect of the stress upon 'soul competency' as the cardinal doctrine of Baptists was to make every man's hat his own church."[22] In his estimation, the principle was derived from the general cultural and religious climate, not from serious Bible study, and is inadequate as a basis for church life. He notes that Southern Baptists achieved "a remarkable degree of cohesiveness and centralized authority" while talking in terms of local autonomy, soul liberty, and private judgment;[23] but this was accomplished "without much reflection" and because of "nontheological factors."[24] These factors were an ecclesiastical structure dating back to 1845 that placed boards and agencies under one Convention, a regional self-consciousness and southern 'mystique,' and a programmatic pragmatism emanating from Nashville.[25]

Though Hudson commented upon Southern and other Baptist groups, his major concern has been for his own fellowship, the American Baptist Churches. After the division from Southern Baptists in 1845,

Baptists of the North perpetuated the society approach, supporting a multiplicity of single purpose societies with little coordination of efforts. The Northern Baptist Convention was not formed until 1907 and was largely a federation of independent societies with few organic ties to one another, the churches, associations, or state conventions. Weakened and fragmented by the fundamentalist movement, this convention was renamed the American Baptist Convention in 1950.

Efforts were made to achieve greater cooperation and coordination, a general secretary was elected, and a central headquarters building at Valley Forge, Pennsylvania, was dedicated in 1962. Many problems remained unsolved, and some were addressed by a Study Commission on Denominational Structure (SCODS) appointed in 1968 and a Study Commission on Relationships (SCOR) created in 1974. The result was a new structure with a new name, The American Baptist Churches in the USA, which became operative on January 1, 1979.[26]

The influence of Hudson has been notable in this shift "back from excessive individualism to Christian responsibility."[27] Repeatedly over several decades he called, through a series of essays, for a shift from a society to a churchly concept. Many of these essays are now available in a single volume, *Baptists in Transition: Individualism and Christian Responsibility.*[28] For Hudson, the Baptist model for responsible church life should be sought not in Anabaptism or separatism but in English Puritanism as expounded by Non-Separatist Independents, adopted with some modification by Particular Baptists, and exhibited in the Philadelphia Baptist Association. This pattern balances independence and interdependence within and among the churches, and the "associational principle" serves as a basis for connectional polity and corporate unity.

The structure that actually emerged among American Baptists, in spite of careful reflection and responsible concern, does not impress an outsider as either biblical or Baptistic at a number of points. A biennial meeting of delegates from congregations and regional organizations has few legislative functions. A general board of about two hundred members serves as the real decision-making body. One member is chosen from each of about one hundred fifty "election districts," which are a new creation, and others at-large by the biennial meeting upon nomination of a committee. The "associational principle" has essentially torpedoed the association.

Members of the General Board are divided into sections that serve as directors of the national program boards. Regional organizations (regional or state conventions or city societies) desiring inclusion in the structure must enter into a Covenant of Relationships. A professional staff functions through a General Staff Council and other councils in administering policies and implementing programs.[29] The churchly concept has overwhelmed the churches.

Although sympathetic with some ideas and concerns expressed by Hudson, Southern Baptists would respond negatively to this representative, semipresbyterian polity. A valid plea for rights does not imply anarchy; nor does the search for responsibility require bureaucracy. An observation by Hudson may prove prophetic for Baptists throughout the nation. "Even the most carefully devised structure is unlikely to provide cohesion unless it is undergirded by the consensus of a common purpose, by a commonly accepted style of doing things arising from common programming, and by loyalty engendered by respected and esteemed leaders."[30]

Missions or Orthodoxy—The Convention Issue

The Southern Baptist Convention was formed "for the purpose of carrying into effect the benevolent intentions of our constituents, by organizing a plan for eliciting, combining and directing the energies of the whole denomination in one sacred effort, for the propagation of the Gospel."[31] The heartbeat of the Convention and the major source of its unity and strength has been a commitment to evangelism and missions. Two mission boards were formed in 1845 and agencies created since that time are regarded as primarily for mission support. Bold Mission Thrust represents no new commitment but a determination and strategy for doing better and more extensively what the Convention has sought to do from the beginning. The Great Commission is taken seriously by Southern Baptists.

The Convention is a functional organization dependent upon voluntary support. It is a servant of the churches. Messengers from the churches adopt policies, approve programs, and establish priorities. The term church is reserved for local congregations and the total body of believers but is never applied to the Convention itself. The latter relates in various ways to churches, associations, state conventions, and other bodies, but none are regarded as inferior or superior. Through the Cooperative Program and designated offerings Southern Baptists share their financial resources for world missions. Primarily in the churches individuals respond to God's call for service, providing personnel for the missionary enterprise, and most often they are nurtured, trained, and supported in many ways for this significant task. Bold Mission Thrust envisions sharing the gospel of Jesus Christ with every person in the world by the year 2000.

A concern for orthodoxy has not been as visible or vocal among Southern Baptists as that to missions. For eight decades the Convention adopted no confessional statement, and orthodoxy was more or less assumed or taken for granted. Some diversity was recognized and accepted, as for example in views on communion or the millennium; flagrant departure from accepted orthodoxy was monitored and dealt with by the Baptist body most integrally involved and affected, in accordance with the standards and procedures of that body. Southern Baptists denied that they were a creedal people, regarded the Bible alone as their sufficient authority for faith and practice, and stressed the need for an open Bible and an open mind in seeking Christian truth.

In the midst of the fundamentalist-modernist controversy the Convention, in 1925, adopted a statement of faith which was a revision and expansion of the New Hampshire Confession. But except for a brief skirmish over implications for the concept of evolution, this confession was largely ignored.[32] Churches and associations as well as Convention agencies and institutions that utilized confessions either formulated their own or adopted some existing statement with an apparent disregard for uniformity.

The Convention expanded rapidly following World War II, and leaders stressed that this success was an evident sign of the blessings of God upon Southern Baptists. From the pulpit and with the pen, Baptists were persuaded that their hour of opportunity had arrived but that if they did not respond faithfully God would discard them and raise up another group. As late as May 1979, Jimmy Allen, then president of the Southern Baptist Convention, sounded this theme. "If we don't respond, God will have to raise up someone else and we (Southern Baptists) will end up on the junk pile of discarded instruments that God is unable to use."[33]

This deeply ingrained conviction has served as a dynamic, compulsive force so that when indicators suggest a slowdown or decline in some aspect of denominational life the result is widespread concern about what has gone wrong. Also, any suggestion for a change in priorities threatens the effective existence of the Convention. President Allen addressed this matter at the Houston Convention (1979), focusing upon the issue under discussion:

As I perceive it, we are being pressed by good and sincere people right now to alter our agenda from Bold Mission Thrust. In this very crucial time of gathering momentum toward increased mission lives, increased mission giving, increased mission praying, some want to change our agenda from missions to orthodoxy. We must resist that temptation.[34]

A number of "good and sincere people" declare that their interest in and commitment to missions is equally intense but that neither missions nor unity must be promoted at the expense of truth, especially truth about the Bible. If such truth is neglected, overlooked, or denied, the God of truth will raise up another group to believe, defend, obey, and spread his Word. The issue of missions or orthodoxy thus clearly involves a people committed both to missions and orthodoxy. Recent confrontations and the examining of priorities, therefore, must be understood in light of events that have transpired over the last two decades which required reflection upon relations between missions and orthodoxy.

Southern Baptists began and ended the sixties and seventies in the midst of controversy. *The Message of Genesis* written by Ralph Elliott, Old Testament professor at Midwestern Seminary, and published by Broadman Press in 1961 offered a "theological" interpretation of Genesis.[35] Elliott, his seminary, and The Sunday School Board came under repeated attack which climaxed in the San Francisco Convention (1962). This Convention appointed a committee (without seminary representatives) to draw up a new confessional statement and adopted resolutions affirming faith in the entire Bible but refused to request that the book be withdrawn from sale. The Sunday School Board decided to let the book go out of print. Elliott sought and found another publisher. He was subsequently dismissed by the seminary trustees. The new "Baptist Faith and Message" was adopted in Kansas City in 1963.

A residue of distrust of the seminaries and The Sunday School Board remained. When a group of religion professors in Baptist colleges criticized *Why I Preach That the Bible Is Literally True* by W. A. Criswell (Broadman, 1969), the colleges were implicated also. But publication of the first volume of a twelve volume *Broadman Bible Commentary* (October 1969) created immediate reaction from many conservatives. G. Henton Davies, principal of Regent's Park College in Oxford, England, and a popular speaker among Southern Baptists, wrote the commentary on Genesis. In interpreting Genesis 22:1-19 Davies indicated that he did not accept literally the command of God to Abraham to sacrifice Isaac.

The Denver Convention in 1970 reverberated with charges and motions concerning the matter, overwhelmingly voting to request The Sunday School Board to withdraw the volume from distribution to be "rewritten with due consideration of the conservative viewpoint."[36] Trustees of the Board reached agreements with the initial authors, principally Davies, for rewriting the materials but the Convention in session the following year called for the dismissal of Davies as a writer of the commentary (St. Louis, 1972). Clyde T. Francisco was then secured by the Board to write the Genesis commentary, which was published in 1973.

Through these and other minor controversies, orthodoxy became a major concern for some Southern Baptists. The Baptist Faith and Message Fellowship was organized in the First Baptist Church of Atlanta, Georgia, in March 1973. This group stressed strict adherence to the 1963 confession as the badge of orthodoxy. The pages of its newspaper highlighted alleged departures therefrom. This organization in turn was criticized for its name, the name of its newspaper, and its repeated attacks upon denominational agencies and personnel.

For a time, strongly conservative groups insisted upon orthodoxy as reflected in the "Baptist Faith and Message," but more recently moderates have taken refuge in this statement as a defensive response also.

Some interpreters have warned against a "creeping creedalism" in Convention life evidenced by repeated adoptions of or appeals to the statement at every level of denominational life. More and more, however, in journals, state papers, and books one issue has emerged as paramount, that of biblical inerrancy. This issue has divided Evangelicals and for many has become the test of orthodoxy.

Independent institutions such as Mid-America Baptist Theological Seminary in Memphis, Tennessee; Luther Rice Seminary in Jacksonville, Florida; and the Criswell Center for Biblical Studies in Dallas, Texas, advertise their total adherance to this view of the Bible. Adrian Rogers, president of the Southern Baptist Convention in 1979-1980, described these schools as "a monument of our failures as Southern Baptists," asserting that they "would not have a breath of a chance to exist if the six Southern Baptist seminaries were committed to biblical inerrancy."[37] Others responded that reasons for their existence are far more complex.

Advocates of inerrancy became more vocal and political in the late seventies, supporting one another in securing key positions and utilizing the preconvention Pastors' Conference as a forum for rallying supporters. Paige Patterson, president of the Criswell Center, and Paul Pressler, a Houston judge, campaigned and organized groups throughout the Convention in preparing to elect a president avowedly committed to biblical inerrancy at Houston in 1979. Adrian Rogers, pastor of the Bellevue Church in Memphis, Tennessee, and an outspoken inerrantist, was elected on the first ballot. Charges of voting irregularities circulated and the Convention censored "overt political activity."[38]

Rogers indicated that he would seek to serve all Southern Baptists and not be controlled by any one group, but he was also reported as asserting that he would not knowingly appoint to any position anyone who was not an inerrantist. The Houston Convention also reaffirmed the statement concerning the Bible in the "Baptist Faith and Message" after moderate spokesmen vocalized an interpretation satisfactory to the inerrantists.[39] The strangely ambivalent Convention also adopted a resolution of appreciation for Southern Baptist seminaries.[40]

Reverberations of the Houston actions occupied the attention of numerous state conventions in the fall of 1979. Charges against col-

leges, editors, and others occupied attention here and there but no deci-
sive victories were recorded by adherants of any one point of view.
Pastor W. A. Criswell and evangelist James Robison continued to spon-
sor a series of Bible conferences designed to rally Southern Baptists in
affirming the Bible as the infallible and inspired Word of God. That the
conflict concerning the Bible has not been put to rest is evident to any
sensitive observer of Southern Baptist life.

Predictions concerning the outcome of this matter would be prema-
ture as the 1980s begin. Southern Baptists without doubt will continue
to promote missions and defend orthodoxy as vital interests. But they
may in time question whether these interests require a business-model
approach geared to success or a political-model approach geared to
power.

God has, indeed, chosen Southern Baptists along with others to share
his gospel with the world. Their motivation for missions must be service
in love, not fear for survival or desire for self-aggrandizement. Likewise,
orthodoxy or "right belief" should be defended against forces of evil that
threaten to envelop our world, but major enemies of truth are not Christian brothers or institutions.

Concluding observations that follow represent an attempt to provide
some perspective for understanding and dealing with this critical issue as
Southern Baptists enter the eighties. First, a review of our denominational heritage should remind us of both the centrality of the Bible and
our aversion to creedalism. For many groups, orthodoxy is defined as
the acceptance of certain creeds: the Augsburg Confession for Luther-
ans; the Westminster Confession for Presbyterians; the Thirty-nine Articles for Anglicans. Baptists rejected this approach, affirming that the
Bible was their authority for faith and practice. Confessions of faith were
never equated with Scripture and could be modified or ignored or abandoned at will. In this context, Baptists declare that they are not a creedal
people. The Bible has been and remains central in Baptist life.

Some Baptists at present define orthodoxy in terms of a particular
view of the Bible. The problem is not in making strong assertions about
the Bible, for Southern Baptists are a people of the Book who believe
and believe in the Bible. The problem is that many assertions imply
underlying assumptions so that to say certain things about the Bible

(some in unbiblical terms) means further to study or not study the Bible in a particular way and come out at preestablished points on a variety of issues. For many Baptists, this approach jeopardizes freedom for which the denomination has struggled and infringes upon the right of any believer to study Scripture for himself in a variety of ways and seek God's leadership in what it means or requires.

Second, the nature of the Convention structure demands that we maintain a system of checks and balances to avoid power struggles. Baptists understand that the freedom described implies responsibilty, especially for those who occupy sensitive positions affecting the lives of others. No Baptist would deny that radical departures from accepted belief and practice should be dealt with, but the question should be where and by whom. For its agencies, the Convention elects trustees and expects that they be trusted. Safeguards are built into Convention procedures for further recourse where needed. Danger arises if these procedures and safeguards are bypassed through the influence of strong personalities or an explosive atmosphere.

In this connection, the pervasiveness of religious controversy should be underscored. Excessive conflict over one issue produces a multiplicity of others. Controversy over one segment of denominational life quickly involves the total denomination. Such controversies reduce denominational effectiveness and compromise the Christian witness.

Third, the need for leadership should remind us of the importance of theological education in denominational life. Every agency except two has changed heads at least once in the past decade. Churches and mission boards have sought and found personnel. Bold Mission Thrust demands trained leaders. From the churches through the colleges, potential leaders arrive at the seminaries for training. Polarization must not begin in the seminaries or over against the seminaries. If some seminaries are labeled as liberal and others as conservative, graduates of those institutions will be characterized in like manner. Also, it is essential that close contact be maintained between the theological schools, denominational leaders, and local churches. They are engaged in a common task and are subservient to the Lord.

Finally, the purpose for which the Convention was formed must remain uppermost. Southern Baptists will continue to debate issues and critique institutions, evaluate policies and criticize practices. May they also agree to disagree in love, maintain Christian standards of honesty and integrity, and focus attention as never before upon "eliciting, combining and directing the energies of the whole denomination in one sacred effort, for the propagation of the Gospel."

Notes

1. H. Richard Niebuhr, *Christ and Culture* (New York: Harper and Brothers Publishers, 1951).
2. Ibid., p. 44.
3. John B. Boles, *The Great Revival 1787-1805* (Lexington, Kentucky: The University Press of Kentucky, 1972), p. 202.
4. Samuel S. Hill, Jr., *Religion and the Solid South* (Nashville: Abingdon Press, 1972), p. 198.
5. Rufus B. Spain, *At Ease in Zion: Social History of Southern Baptists 1865-1900* (Nashville: Vanderbilt University Press, 1961), p. 214.
6. Ibid.
7. John Lee Eighmy, *Churches in Cultural Captivity: A History of the Social Attitudes of Southern Baptists* (Knoxville: The University of Tennessee Press, 1972), pp. 207-208.
8. Ibid., p. X.
9. Ibid., p. XI.
10. Foy Valentine, "Baptist Polity and Social Pronouncements," *Baptist History and Heritage* XIV (July, 1979), pp. 52-61.
11. Ibid., p. 54.
12. Ibid.
13. Ibid., p. 61.
14. W. T. Whitley, *A History of British Baptists* (London: Charles Griffin and Company, Limited, 1923), p. 4.
15. H. Wheeler Robinson, *Baptist Principles* (London: The Carey Kingsgate Press, 1925).
16. Henry Cook, *What Baptists Stand For* (London: The Carey Kingsgate Press, 1947), p. 18.
17. E. Y. Mullins, *The Axioms of Religion* (Philadelphia: American Baptist Publication Society, 1908), p. 59.
18. Ibid., pp. 73-74.
19. Winthrop S. Hudson, *Baptists in Transition: Individualism and Christian Responsibility* (Valley Forge: Judson Press, 1979), p. 142.

20. Herschel H. Hobbs and E. Y. Mullins, *The Axioms of Religion,* Revised Edition (Nashville: Broadman Press, 1978), p. 163.
21. Ibid.
22. Hudson, p. 142.
23. Ibid., p. 148.
24. Ibid.
25. Ibid., pp. 148-149.
26. For an excellent description of the entire process see Robert T. Handy, "American Baptist Polity: What's Happening and Why," *Baptist History and Heritage* XIV (July, 1979), pp. 12-21, 51.
27. Robert T. Handy, "Foreword," in Winthrop S. Hudson, *Baptists in Transition: Individualism and Christian Responsibility* (Valley Forge: Judson Press, 1979), p. 14.
28. Except for the "Foreword" by Handy and the "Afterword" by Hudson, the essays were previously published in journals and books cited in the volume.
29. The article by Handy in *Baptist History and Heritage* and cited above describes the structure.
30. Hudson, p. 155.
31. See Robert A. Baker, *A Baptist Source Book* (Nashville: Broadman Press, 1966), p. 116.
32. See William Wright Barnes, *The Southern Baptist Convention: A Study in the Development of Ecclesiology* (Seminary Hill, Texas: Published by the author, 1934), p. 8 and Walter B. Shurden, "The Problem of Authority in the Southern Baptist Convention," *Review and Expositor* LXXV (Spring, 1978), p. 228.
33. *Baptist Standard,* 30 May 1979, p. 3.
34. *The Baptist Record,* 28 June 1979, p. 2.
35. Ralph H. Elliott, *The Message of Genesis* (Nashville: Broadman Press, 1961).
36. *Annual,* SBC, 1970, p. 63.
37. *Baptist Standard,* 20 June 1979, p. 5.
38. *Annual,* SBC, 1979, p. 58.
39. *Baptist Standard,* 20 June 1979, p. 5.
40. *Annual,* SBC, 1979, p. 55.

About the Cover

Scene 1 (top left) illustrates the spirit of cooperation that characterizes Baptists. This drawing depicts the formation of the Philadelphia Association in 1707.

Scene 2 (bottom left) illustrates an experience of the baptism of believers. Under cover of darkness, 9 converts were baptized in the James River near Chesterfield, Virginia, in 1773.

Scene 3 (right) illustrates the significance of religious liberty for Baptists. George W. Truett is shown making a major statement on this theme on the steps of the nation's Capitol in 1920.

This artwork is by Erwin M. Hearne, Jr. The cover was designed by Gene Elliott. These drawings and other illustrations of Baptist heritage also appear in Albert McClellan, *Meet Southern Baptists* (Nashville: Broadman Press, 1978).